JOGGING

About the Authors

Garth Fisher is the Director of the Human Performance Research Center and Professor of Physical Education at Brigham Young University. He has done much research in the area of fitness and has published numerous articles and papers. He has authored the book, *Your Heart Rate: The Key to Real Fitness,* and co-authored the books, *Scientific Basis of Athletic Conditioning, Jogging, The Complete Book of Physical Fitness,* and *How to Lower Your Fat Thermostat.* He also writes a weekly column about fitness for *The Deseret News.*

Active in professional affairs, he has been chairman of the research section for the SW District AAHPERD and UAHPERD, and is a fellow in the American College of Sports Medicine. He is also certified as a "Program Director" by the ACSM to direct exercise programs for high risk and post-cardiac patients. He presently serves as Chairman of the Utah Governor's Council of Physical Fitness.

Dr. Fisher lectures regularly on the various aspects of fitness and weight control to both professional and non-professional groups and is sought out as a consultant for developing fitness programs and facilities. He earned his undergraduate degree at Brigham Young University, his M.A. from Sacramento State College, and his Ph.D. from the University of New Mexico.

Dr. Philip E. Allsen, currently a Professor of Physical Education at Brigham Young University, has been active in many aspects of physical education. He earned his B.S. at Ricks College, M.S. at Brigham Young University, and Ed.D. at the University of Utah, all with honors. He has held positions at all three schools and has also served as athletic director for the city of Gardena, California, and as a Physical Fitness Officer in the U.S. Navy. Dr. Allsen has held his present position for the past 10 years. He holds honors and memberships in many professional organizations, ranging from AAHPERD to Nutrition Today Society. In addition to co-authoring *Jogging,* he has co-authored two editions of *Racquetball/Paddleball* and singly authored *Fitness for Life* for WCB.

JOGGING

A. Garth Fisher
Brigham Young University

Philip E. Allsen
Brigham Young University

Second Edition

ꞣꞔb
Wm. C. Brown Publishers
Dubuque, Iowa

Contributing Editor

Aileene Lockhart
Texas Woman's University

Cover photograph © Jean-Claude Lejeune

Library of Congress Catalog Card Number: 86–72895

ISBN 0–697–07241–X

Printed in the United States of America
10 9 8 7 6 5 4 3 2 1

Contents

Preface

Jogging has become an important part of the lifestyle of literally millions of Americans. To some it has become an addiction. To others, only a daily "fad" that cannot be ignored. But to most it has become a wonderful part of life. The reasons for the increasing popularity of this activity, which involves no ball or implements, no team vs. team, nor cheering crowds, but which requires both effort and sweat, are difficult to explain but become obvious after one begins a regular routine of jogging.

The seriousness of the health problems associated with inactivity are clearly documented. However, the increasing popularity of jogging cannot be a result of the fear of dying. If this were so, no one would smoke cigarettes. No, the explanation is much more complex than this.

Once a person has jogged for a few months, some remarkable changes begin to occur; bodies become lean and tight, eyes are clear, the heart beats strong and slow; running up stairs is no longer a terrible experience in fatigue.

But even beyond the changes which occur in the body, is the exhilaration that accompanies this change in activity. Dr. George Sheehan, noted cardiologist and writer, explained, "For 15 years I have been a distance runner, and I'm still trying to explain this self-renewing inner compulsion. But the more I run, the more I want to run. And the more I run, the more I live a life conditioned by my running." He started running for the same reasons many of us do; to get into shape, to improve appearance, to prevent a heart attack, and to add years to life. Like many others, the original reasons for running became dim. Running or jogging is more than "fitness and a trim body, more than weight loss and muscles revived." Running was a total experience. It has become part of his lifestyle.

In this revised text the authors will take readers through an easy-to-understand program that starts at a beginner's level and then progresses to a level where, if they wish, they could even run a marathon on a competitive basis.

Readers will be able to obtain information concerning the selection of equipment to get started. Simple tests to determine the current level of fitness are presented and then jogging guidelines that are self-monitored are explained. In a short period of time the reader not only knows "why" he or she should jog, but will be able to know "how" to jog using a personalized type of program.

In the 2nd edition, we have included completely updated chapters on weight control and nutrition. The new chapters are exciting because they explain why dieting alone has been so ineffective, and give up-to-the-minute guidelines for losing weight by jogging and eating properly. In these chapters, you will finally understand why jogging is so important for weight control and that the *type* of food rather than the quantity is the culprit in obesity. You will also learn how to eat to help to avoid heart disease and certain cancers. We have also included new tables for determining the amount of fat on your body. These tables are extremely accurate and quite easy to use.

The topic of flexibility is also explained and simple stretching exercises that will help to alleviate joint and connective tissue problems are demonstrated.

One of the outstanding features of this text is the question and answer section. The authors have tabulated, over many years, questions that have been asked by the thousands of people they have assisted in exercise programs and provided answers that are understandable by others who might have the same problems.

Why jog? Jogging is the simplest and most natural of all the ways to fitness. It is a life style. It is the return of man to carefree days of play and freedom. For that hour each day, we do what we really want to do and enjoy it. All of the changes which occur to the body from jogging are a bonus.

In the 2nd Ed of this book, we would like to help you experience the great rewards of jogging with understanding and with safety. We hope that this experience will change your life as it has changed the lives of many before you.

1 Getting Started

The purpose of this chapter is to give you, the reader, some practical guidelines to becoming a jogger. These will be useful to you immediately and will help you to solve many problems in the future if used as you begin your jogging program.

PHYSICAL EXAMINATION

Most young, healthy persons can begin a jogging program safely. Of course, anyone who is doubtful about his or her state of health, regardless of age, should consult with a physician before beginning a rigorous program. There are some authorities who believe, in principle at least, that there is less risk in activity than in continuous inactivity. In their opinion, there is more need to undergo a careful medical examination if you intend to be sedentary than if you decide to begin an exercise program, in order to determine whether your health is good enough to stand the inactivity (5). The Connecticut Mutual Life Insurance Company has compiled a screening questionnaire for people who are considering exercise programs. If you answer "yes" to any of the following questions, then you should check with your doctor. There is a possibility that a medical problem could hamper your fitness program. Remember, an ounce of prevention is worth a pound of cure!

1. Have you ever had pains or a sensation of pressure in your chest that occurred with exertion, lasted a few minutes, and then subsided with resting?
2. Do you get chest discomfort when climbing stairs, walking against a cold wind, or during any physical (including sexual) or emotional activity?
3. Does your heart ever beat unevenly or irregularly or seem to flutter or skip beats?
4. Do you have sudden bursts of very rapid heart action or periods of very slow heart action without apparent cause?
5. Do you take any prescription medicine on a regular basis?
6. Has your electrocardiogram at rest or during exercise ever been abnormal?
7. Do you have any respiratory problems, such as emphysema, asthma, wheezing, chronic bronchitis, or do you experience an unusual breathlessness or exertion that is more than that experienced by others doing the same thing?
8. Do you have arthritis, rheumatism, gout, or any condition affecting your joints?
9. Do you have any orthopedic problems affecting your feet, ankles, knees, or hips that cause pain or limit your motion in any way?

10. Do you have a bad back, a sacroiliac, or a disc problem?
11. Do you have any known cardiac condition that might prohibit an exercise program?
12. Are you aware of any risk factors, such as high blood pressure (hypertension), overweight (by more than 30%), diabetes, or high blood-fat levels? Are you a heavy smoker? Do your relatives have a history of heart disease?

The American College of Sports Medicine has recommended the following general guidelines for individuals who wish to begin an exercise program (1):

1. If you are under 45 years of age, and have no known coronary heart-disease risk factors nor previous history of cardiovascular disease, you may begin an exercise program safely without special medical clearance. However, if you haven't had a medical examination during the past two years or if you have any questions concerning your health status, see your physician prior to beginning your program.
2. If you are 35 years old or older, it would be advisable to have a medical evaluation prior to any major increase in activity level, if you have a history of cardiovascular disease or a combination of cardiovascular disease risk factors. (Appendix 1—Risk Factors)

Jogging does not require a great amount of expensive equipment, but in order to prevent injuries and irritations to the body, some basic information is needed.

EQUIPMENT

Shoes

The key to your jogging program is the selection of a good pair of shoes. Shoes will not make you a great runner; only a proper training program will bring this about, but shoes can eliminate many of the hazards of jogging, such as blisters, shock to the feet, and lower leg and hip pain. Since you will be running hundreds of miles in the shoes you purchase, you should select your shoes as you would a good friend. Canvas tennis shoes are not good for jogging, because they are too heavy and usually give poor foot support. Even though a good pair of shoes may appear to be expensive, jogging is still a relatively inexpensive sport over a long period of time. When you project the price of shoes over the time they last, the cost is less than 10 to 15 cents a day.

There is a wide variety of good shoes available, but in order to purchase a pair wisely, you should understand what factors contribute to the construction of jogging shoes. It is unfortunate that most of the important components of a shoe, such as structure and quality of material, are not visible to the buyer. When you decide to purchase a pair of jogging shoes, you should carefully examine the sole, heel, inside of the shoe, and the weight of the shoe. Figure 1.1 contains a diagram of some basic features of a training shoe.

Sole   The sole is important because it provides the runner with traction, shock absorption, flexibility, and protection. The sole is actually composed of two layers.

The outer layer must be durable because it makes contact with the running surface. The middle sole must be soft and pliable to act as a shock absorber.

Another feature to check is the flexibility of the sole: this can be done very easily by bending the shoe. If it is stiff and inflexible, you will be inviting foot and leg problems if you buy it. The wedge of the sole should end at a point on the shoe where the foot flexes, in order to allow for proper flexion, since the front one-third of the foot is where the roll off the toe occurs while running. If the shoe isn't flexible in this area, considerable stress will be placed on the feet and legs.

Heel   It is important that the heel be elevated in order to reduce the stress on the legs. For most people, the heel should be about a half-inch higher than the sole. The heel area should be well supported by what is known as the "counter" or the part that surrounds the heel. The counter should be firm and padded on the top rim in order to prevent undue movement of the heel while jogging. Also, check the extension of the heel which contacts the Achilles tendon. It should give support but should not create an excessive amount of friction or pressure on the tendon.

Inside the Shoe   It is mandatory that the inner material does not irritate the foot by creating friction problems when you run. Move your hands around the inside of the shoe to determine if there are any rough edges or seams that might rub against the foot. The insole of the shoe should be soft and smooth so that it will not irritate the foot.

Most shoes have either a built-in arch support or a piece of sponge rubber glued to the inside of the shoe. The best way to check this feature is to put the shoes on and jog around the store to determine how the arch feels.

The upper portion of the shoe should be a material that gives good support but does not irritate the feet (usually nylon or leather). Check the shoe to make sure the toe box has enough room for your toes to spread out and be comfortable.

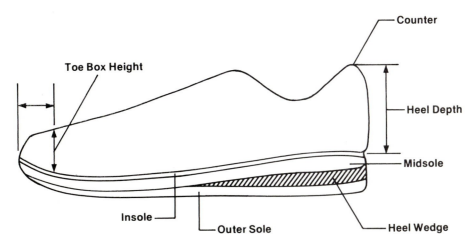

FIGURE 1–1 Features of the training shoe.

Your big toes should be about three-quarters of an inch short of the front of the shoe to avoid pressure while running. Also check the height of the toe box to make sure it is high enough to prevent unnecessary rubbing on the top of the toes. The sides of the shoe should firmly enclose the rest of the foot to reduce movement within the shoe which will cause blisters.

When you go to buy your jogging shoes, wear a pair of the socks you'll wear while running, so that the fit of the shoe will be the same.

Weight   Many people who are just starting to jog look for an ultra-light shoe worn by world-class runners in competition and conclude that this is the best shoe to purchase for their training program. The few ounces that might be saved by sacrificing support and shock absorption qualities are not worth the price of foot and leg injuries. Most of the top shoe brands are comparable in weight, therefore the features of sole, heel, and inside of shoe construction are more important.

By following these simple guidelines, you should be able intelligently to buy a pair of jogging shoes. However, the final test is when you put the shoes on your feet. They should immediately feel comfortable. Any initial discomfort will be magnified when your feet strike the running surface some 800 times a mile.

Runner's World magazine each year has a special issue devoted to the rating of shoes.* It would be worth your time to check this rating. In conjunction with this survey, panelists were asked to supply an "ideal" measurement for several key parts of a shoe. They were also asked to rate the importance of the individual parts of the shoe's anatomy, as "very important," meaning it is an essential feature in the selection of a shoe; "important," meaning it is nice but not essential; or "not important."

The results of this survey are as follows:

Item	Rating
Flexibility under the forefoot	very important
Rigid heel counter, covering the full heel area	very important
Soft padding at the achilles tendon and ankle area	important
Removable sponge arch support	important
Built-in arch support	important
Variable widths	important
Upper material that is soft at the start and stays soft	important
Lacing pattern	not important
Last on which the shoe is built	very important
Overall quality and construction	very important
Tread pattern	important
Rounded heel shape	important
Rounded toe shape	important

Specific suggestions for the measurement of key features of a training shoe for jogging were also made by the panel.

Feature	Suggested Measurement	
	Inches	*Centimeters*
Thickness of sole, measured under the ball of foot.	.55	1.40
Heel height, measured at point of maximum thickness	.99	2.51
Heel depth, from insole to top of achilles pad	2.9	7.37
Heel depth, from insole to top of outside ankle pad	1.9	4.83
Heel depth, from insole to top of inside ankle pad	2.2	5.59
Heel width, at widest point	3.2	8.13
Toe box height, measured at one inch from outside top of shoe	1.2	3.05

How do your jogging shoes rate? Take a tape measure and compare the dimensions of your shoes with the measurements recommended by Runner's World *panelists.*

Socks

The chief reason for wearing socks is to prevent blisters. You may see some people who jog without socks, but they take a chance of developing foot irritation. Some runners obtain good results by wearing a thin pair of cotton socks against the foot and a heavier pair over them to reduce the rubbing of the foot against the inside of the shoe. The type of sock you choose will be determined by personal choice and the needs of your feet.

Shorts—Shirt—Warm-ups

The principal recommendation in this area is to wear clothes that are loose fitting and comfortable. If your clothing rubs and chafes the body, it will soon take the pleasure out of your jogging program. If you do experience chafing, use some petroleum jelly on the skin before you begin jogging to stop the irritation.

If you find it necessary to wear a warm-up suit because of the weather, be sure it will absorb the perspiration but will also be loose enough to allow the body heat to escape. Since you warm up very quickly while running, this is an important consideration. The key parts of the body to keep warm are the hands and the head since the arms, legs, and trunk generate a relatively large amount of heat and do not require as much protection while running on cold days.

With the procurement of your jogging equipment, you are now prepared with all of the essentials to change your life by embarking on a life-long road to fitness.

FITNESS TESTING

Two excellent fitness tests are included to help you evaluate your fitness level. The purpose of fitness testing is two fold: (1) an initial fitness evaluation will help you decide what level of activity is best for you, and (2) subsequent tests will allow you to evaluate your progress as you continue your jogging program.

If you have been completely inactive for the past year, we recommend that you walk for several weeks (following the time schedule in Table 2–1) before taking either test. If you have been fairly active, but your activity has been sporadic in nature, we recommend you take the submaximal *"Sharkeys' Test"* rather than Cooper's 1.5 mile run. The Cooper's test may be used by anyone who exercises regularly and can jog for 15 minutes or so without stopping.

A description of each test follows:

Forest Service Step Test: (11)

The Forest Service step test developed by Dr. Brian Sharkey is an excellent test for the average inactive person since it is a "submaximal" test of fitness. This means that it is designed to test your fitness level without forcing your body to maximal level of stress such as might be experienced in a 1.5 miles all-out run.

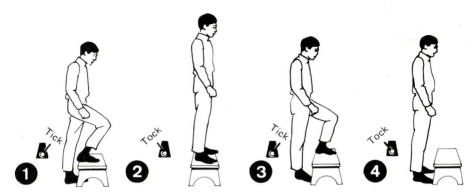

FIGURE 1–2 Stepping sequence for the Forest Service Step Test. (From Sharkey, B. J. *Physiological Fitness and Weight Control,* Mountain Press Publishing Co., Missoula, p. 106)

You will need a stool or chair 15¾ inches high for men and 13 inches high for women, a stop watch or at least a watch with a second hand, and a metronome. It would be a good idea to practice counting your pulse before you begin the test. You can feel the pulse at the base of either thumb on the inside soft area of the wrist (radial artery) or at the temple near the upper front part of the ear (temporal artery). The carotid artery in the neck could also be used. However, pressure on this artery sometimes causes a decrease in pulse rate and could yield inaccurate results.

Practice taking pulse counts for a series of 10 second intervals on the left radial artery of a third person while your partner simultaneously counts the pulse of the person's right wrist. Compare scores after each ten second time period. Are your scores consistently within 3 beats of each other? Two beats? One beat?

Begin by stepping up and down on the stool or chair at 90 steps per minute in keeping with the metronome. You step up on the first beat with one leg, bring the other leg up on the second to a full standing position on the stool, return the first leg to the floor on the third beat, and then back to the floor with the other foot on the fourth beat (fig. 1–2). You may alternate the lead leg during the test, but continue to step up and down for the entire five minutes.

When five minutes of stepping have elapsed, sit down and count your own pulse, or have someone count it for exactly 15 seconds, beginning exactly 15 seconds from the end of the test. Multiply the number of beats you count for that 15 second period by 4 and enter the product into Table 1–1 a and b. Read your predicted fitness capacity across from your weight. This figure is expressed as milliliters of oxygen per kilogram body weight and indicates the amount of energy you can produce at maximum work.

TABLE 1–1A FITNESS INDEX—MEN

Body Weight

Post Exercise Pulse	120	130	140	150	160	170	180	190	200	210	220	230	240	
180	33.0	32.8	32.8	32.6	32.6	32.3	32.3	32.3	32.3	32.1	32.1	31.9	31.9	180
175	34.8	33.9	33.9	33.7	33.4	33.4	33.4	33.0	33.0	33.0	32.8	32.8	32.8	175
170	35.4	34.8	34.8	34.8	34.3	34.3	34.3	34.3	34.1	34.1	34.1	34.1	34.1	170
165	36.7	36.7	35.9	35.6	35.6	35.6	35.2	35.2	35.2	35.2	35.0	34.8	34.8	165
160	37.2	37.2	37.2	37.2	37.0	36.7	36.7	36.7	36.5	36.5	36.5	35.9	35.9	160
155	38.7	38.5	38.3	38.1	37.8	37.8	37.8	37.8	37.8	37.8	37.6	37.4	37.4	155
150	40.3	39.8	39.8	39.6	38.9	38.9	38.9	38.9	38.7	38.7	38.7	38.7	38.5	150
145	41.6	40.9	40.7	40.3	40.3	40.3	40.0	40.0	40.0	40.0	40.0	40.0	40.0	145
140	42.9	42.7	42.0	41.8	41.8	41.8	41.6	41.6	41.6	41.6	41.6	41.6	41.6	140
135	44.4	44.0	43.3	43.1	43.1	43.1	43.1	43.1	43.1	42.9	42.9	42.7	42.5	135
130	46.2	45.8	45.5	45.3	45.1	44.9	44.9	44.9	44.7	44.7	44.7	44.2	44.2	130
125	48.0	47.3	47.1	46.9	46.6	46.6	46.6	46.6	46.4	46.4	46.4	46.4	46.4	125
120	49.7	49.3	49.1	48.8	48.6	48.6	48.4	48.4	48.4	48.4	48.4	48.4	48.4	120
115	51.7	51.7	51.5	51.0	51.0	51.0	51.0	51.0	50.6	50.6	50.6	50.4	49.5	115
110	53.7	53.7	53.5	53.2	53.2	53.0	52.8	52.8	52.8	52.6	52.6	51.7	51.3	110
105	56.1	56.1	56.1	55.7	55.4	55.2	55.2	55.0	55.0	55.0	53.9	53.5	53.0	105
100	59.0	58.7	58.3	58.1	58.1	58.1	57.4	57.4	57.6	56.5	56.1	55.3		100
95	64.2	61.8	61.2	61.2	61.2	60.9	60.7	60.7	59.4	58.7	57.2			95
90	67.3	65.1	64.7	64.7	64.5	64.2	64.0	62.5	61.6	60.1				90
85	69.3	69.3	68.2	67.8	67.8	67.8	65.8	64.9	63.7					85
80	72.8	72.6	71.9	71.9	71.9	69.5	68.4	67.2						80
	120	130	140	150	160	170	180	190	200	210	220	230	240	

Adjust your fitness capacity by your age in Table 1–2. Since heart rate decreases slightly each year you live, you must adjust the heart rate response to exercise by this factor, if you are over 35 or under 15 years of age. The adjusted fitness capacity can be entered into Table 1–3 a or b to indicate your fitness category.

Cooper's Test: (7)

Dr. Kenneth Cooper found a correlation between the time it takes to run 1.5 miles and your ability to produce energy aerobically (with oxygen). His test is based upon this correlation and can easily be administered by running 1.5 miles on some high school track, in a park, or along a street where the distance is measured out with your car. Table 1–4 shows your fitness category based upon the amount of time it takes you to cover that distance.

This test should *not* be taken by people who are completely inactive, people over 35 years of age without a doctor's clearance, or by anyone who has a past history of heart disease or any of the major heart disease risk factors.

TABLE 1–1B   FITNESS INDEX—WOMEN

Body Weight

Post Exercise Pulse	80	90	100	110	120	130	140	150	160	170	180	190	
175												31.2	175
170				31.9	31.9	32.1	32.1	32.1	32.1	32.1	32.1	32.3	170
165				32.3	32.6	33.0	33.0	33.2	33.2	33.2	33.2	33.2	165
160			33.4	33.7	33.9	34.1	34.3	34.3	34.3	34.3	34.3	34.3	160
155			34.5	34.8	35.2	35.4	35.4	35.4	35.4	35.4	35.4	35.4	155
150			35.6	36.1	36.3	36.3	36.7	36.7	36.7	36.7	36.7	36.7	150
145		37.2	37.4	38.1	38.1	38.1	38.1	38.1	38.3	38.3	38.9	38.9	145
140		38.7	39.4	39.4	39.4	39.6	39.6	39.6	39.6	39.6	39.6	39.6	140
135	39.6	39.8	40.0	40.3	40.3	40.9	40.9	41.1	41.1	41.4	41.6	41.6	135
130	40.5	41.1	41.8	42.0	42.2	42.9	42.9	43.1	43.3	43.3	43.6	43.6	130
125	41.4	43.6	43.8	44.0	44.0	44.4	44.7	44.9	44.9	45.3	45.3	45.3	125
120	42.5	45.3	45.8	46.0	46.0	46.4	46.9	47.1	47.1	47.3	47.5	47.5	120
115	44.4	47.7	48.0	48.0	48.0	48.0	49.3	49.3	49.3	49.3	49.3	49.3	115
110	48.0	50.2	51.5	51.7	51.7	51.7	51.9	52.4	52.4	52.8			110
105	51.7	53.7	53.7	53.9	54.1	54.6	55.4	55.7	55.7				105
100	55.2	56.8	57.0	57.6	58.3	58.3	59.4						100
95	58.1	60.7	61.2	61.6	62.3	62.3							95
90	62.7	64.7	65.6	67.5	67.5	68.6							90
	80	90	100	110	120	130	140	150	160	170	180	190	

From Sharkey, B. J. *Physiological Fitness and Weight Control,* Mountain Press Publishing Co., Missoula, p. 106.

TABLE 1–2   AGE ADJUSTMENT GUIDELINES
(Multiply your predicted VO_2 max by the age factors before entering table 2–5.)

Age	Factor
15	1.1
25	1.0
35	0.87
40	0.83
45	0.78
50	0.75
55	0.71
60	0.68
65	0.65

Source: Sharkey, B. J., *Physiological Fitness and Weight Control,* Mountain Press Publishing Co., Missoula, Montana, p. 106.

TABLE 1–3A   MEN'S FITNESS RATING

Nearest Age	Superior	Excellent	Very Good	Good	Fair	Poor	Very Poor
25	55	50	45	40	35	30	25
35	53	48	43	38	33	28	23
45	51	46	41	36	31	26	21
55	49	44	39	34	29	24	19
65	47	42	37	32	27	22	17

TABLE 1–3B   WOMEN'S FITNESS RATING

Nearest Age	Superior	Excellent	Very Good	Good	Fair	Poor	Very Poor
25	52	47	42	37	32	27	22
35	50	45	40	35	30	25	20
45	48	43	38	33	28	23	18
55	46	41	36	31	26	21	16
65	44	39	34	29	24	20	15

Source: Sharkey, B. J., *Physiological Fitness and Weight Control,* Mountain Press Publishing Co., Missoula, Montana, p. 109.

This is an excellent test for young, active people, or older people who have been cleared for activity by their physician and who have been exercising for several months. Be sure to stop the test if you experience excessive fatigue, shortness of breath, light-headedness, nausea, or any pain in the chest or upper arm.

What information would you want to obtain before advising a friend whether to take the Forest Service step test or Cooper test of fitness?

TABLE 1-4 1.5 MILE RUN TEST TIME (MINUTES)

Fitness Category		13–19	20–29	30–39	40–49	50–59	60+
					Age (Years)		
I. Very poor	(Men)	>15:31*	>16:01	>16:31	>17:31	>19:01	>20:01
	(Women)	>18:31	>19:01	>19:31	>20:01	>20:31	>21:01
II. Poor	(Men)	12:11–15:30	14:01–16:00	14:44–16:30	15:36–17:30	17:01–19:00	19:01–20:00
	(Women)	18:30–16:55	19:00–18:31	19:30–19:01	20:00–19:31	20:30–20:01	21:00–21:31
III. Fair	(Men)	10:49–12:10	12:01–14:00	12:31–14:45	13:01–15:35	14:31–17:00	16:16–19:00
	(Women)	16:54–14:31	18:30–15:55	19:00–16:31	19:30–17:31	20:00–19:01	20:30–19:31
IV. Good	(Men)	9:41–10:48	10:46–12:00	11:01–12:30	11:31–13:00	12:31–14:30	14:00–16:15
	(Women)	14:30–12:30	15:54–13:31	16:30–14:31	17:30–15:56	19:00–16:31	19:30–17:31
V. Excellent	(Men)	8:37–9:40	9:45–10:45	10:00–11:00	10:30–11:30	11:00–12:30	11:15–13:59
	(Women)	12:29–11:50	13:30–12:30	14:30–13:00	15:55–13:45	16:30–14:30	17:30–16:30
VI. Superior	(Men)	<8:37	<9:45	<10:00	<10:30	<11:00	<11:15
	(Women)	<11:50	<12:30	<13:00	<13:45	<14:30	<16:30

*<Means "less than"; > means "more than."

Source: *The Aerobics Way* by Kenneth H. Cooper, M.D., M.Ph. Copyright © 1977 by Kenneth H. Cooper. Reprinted by permission of the publisher M. Evans and Company, Inc., New York, New York 10017.

2 *Jogging Guidelines*

We assume that you have had your physical examination, purchased your jogging gear and are ready to embark upon a jogging program. Many problems can be eliminated by learning a few basic "rules of the road" before starting. "The average American," according to Dr. Kenneth Cooper of the Aerobics Institute, "takes 20 years to get out of condition, and wants to get back in shape in 20 days. You can't do it. If your heart tolerates it, your legs won't."

The guidelines that follow are the basic principles needed to formulate a sound jogging program. It is the best available advice that research indicates on how to jog effectively. Following these "rules" or guidelines will result in a jogging program which will be sure to cause the proper kinds of physiological changes to occur.

INTENSITY

One of the most important guidelines for jogging is to use the proper intensity. Intensity refers to the vigor of your exercise period. Much research has been done to determine how vigorously you must jog in order to cause effective aerobic changes. The findings are that changes in cardiovascular fitness are directly related to the intensity or vigor of your exercise. The more intense the exercise, the better the training effect. Athletes often train at or near maximum intensity as they prepare for competition. They can also run four minute miles and perform other feats which cannot be accomplished by the average person. It is important to realize that the average person can obtain a fine training effect at a much lower intensity level than the athlete and should train at a lower intensity for both safety and comfort. The question, then, is how intense should activity be to yield a good training effect without being so tough that exercise is no fun?

Most exercise physiologists agree that the physiological and biochemical changes associated with training occur at intensities equal to about 70 percent of an individual's maximum aerobic capacity. Intensities less than 60 percent are not nearly as effective (1,9).

How can you tell if you are at 60 or 70 percent of your maximum aerobic capacity? Fortunately, these levels can be estimated, using the heart rate as a guide. Research has shown that heart rate, expressed as a percent of maximum heart rate, is significantly related to percent maximum aerobic capacity. The relationship is shown in Figure 2–1. Note that 60 percent maximum aerobic capacity is related to 72 percent maximum heart rate and that 80 percent maximum

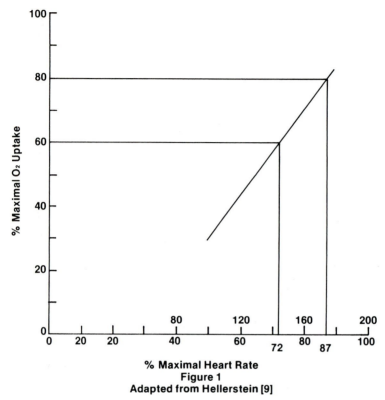

% Maximal O₂ Uptake

80   120   160   200

0   20   20   40   60   80   100
                           72   87

% Maximal Heart Rate
Figure 1
Adapted from Hellerstein [9]

FIGURE 2–1 Percent maximal heart
rate and percent maximal O_2 uptake
relationships.

aerobic capacity is related to 87 percent maximum heart rate. This relationship
is valid regardless of your work capacity; it allows you to measure your own intensity by monitoring your heart rate.

Maximum heart rate can be predicted using the formula 220 − age =
maximum heart rate. Of course, the predicted value may be slightly different for
you than for another person of the same age, since there are other factors besides
age which affect maximum heart rate. However, using this information, you can
compute the approximate training heart-rate range for a person of any age by
multiplying the predicted maximum heart rate by the recommended heart rate
percent for effective training.

When you begin jogging, you will probably want to work at an intensity of
about 70 percent of your maximum heart rate. After you have jogged for several
months, you will be comfortable at about 80 percent. This is the intensity that
most joggers prefer (8). Well-conditioned joggers may increase their heart rate
until it is 85 to 90 percent of their maximum, but they will be limited to jogging
shorter distances at this intensity.

		70%	80%	90%	Max Predicted H.R.
	20	140	160	180	200
	25	135	156	175	195
	30	133	152	171	190
	35	129	148	165	185
	40	126	144	162	180
Age	45	122	140	157	175
in	50	119	136	153	170
Years	55	115	132	148	165
	60	112	128	144	160
	65	108	124	139	155
	70	105	120	135	150

FIGURE 2–2 Percent maximum predicted heart rate per minute for various ages.

Figure 2–2 shows the heart rate at 70, 80, and 90 percent for people of different ages. You should use these heart rates as a guide for proper training intensity as you become a jogger.

How to Monitor Your Heart Rate

To determine your level of intensity accurately, you must learn to count your pulse. You can feel the pulse in many different areas of the body. One of the easiest places to feel it is at the base of your thumb in the soft area of the wrist. You can also feel it just in front of the ear at the temple or in the carotid arteries of the neck next to your voice box. However, it's probably better to monitor the wrist or the temple since pressure on the arteries of the neck can cause a slowing of heart rate which may yield an inaccurate count.

Practice counting your heart rate at rest for one minute. It is interesting to note that many great endurance athletes have resting pulse rates as low as 40–45 beats per minute. This low, strong resting pulse indicates a very efficient heart muscle which has been developed through many years of training. Your own resting heart rate will decrease after you have exercised for two or three months and your heart muscle becomes more efficient as a pump.

Practice counting your heart rate after you have walked around briskly for about a minute. Notice how much faster your heart is beating now? This response is normal. The harder you work, the faster the heart beats.

If you practice a little, you will soon learn how to count your pulse while walking, but you will find it difficult to count while jogging. Luckily, the heart rate immediately after jogging (within 10 to 15 seconds) is nearly the same as it was during the jog. Therefore, you can estimate your jogging heart rate by counting the pulse for 10 seconds immediately after your jog and multiplying it by six. An even easier method is to use Figure 2–3. This figure shows the *ten second* heart rate at 70, 80, and 90 percent for people of different ages. You can

		70%	80%	90%
	20	23	27	30
	25	22	26	29
	30	22	25	28
Age	35	21	25	27
in	40	21	24	27
Years	45	20	23	26
	50	20	23	25
	55	19	22	25
	60	19	21	24
	65	18	21	23
	70	17	20	22

FIGURE 2–3 Percent maximum
predicted heart rate in 10 seconds for
various ages.

think of this 10 second heart rate as your "target heart rate." For instance, if
you are 20 years old, and are just beginning to jog, you would choose 23 as your
"target." This is the same as 144 divided by 6 and represents your 70 percent
maximum heart rate level. After warming up, you would jog for one or two minutes at an easy pace, then slow to a walk, and count your pulse for 10 seconds.
If your 10 second count was 21, you would know that you should increase the
intensity of your jogging slightly. If the 10 second count were 26, you could slow

down slightly during your next jogging period. You should continue to check your heart rate from time to time until you recognize the sensations in your body which indicate the proper intensity of exercise.

As you become more trained, you will establish a new target heart rate of about 80 percent of your maximum heart rate. Later, you may even work at higher intensities.

One of the great advantages of jogging using a target heart rate is that you can jog effectively under many different conditions. For instance, exercise in intense heat requires more energy than exercise at moderate temperatures. If you try to maintain your usual speed, your heart rate will go too high, and you would be unable to continue for very long. However, if you monitor your heart rate, you will slow down your speed and still get the same training effect. High altitude exercise creates the same problem. If you were to run a mile in Mexico City at the same speed you ran at sea level, you would have a much higher heart rate.

This principle works the other way too. As your cardiovascular system becomes more efficient, work will become easier for you, and you will be forced to increase the speed you run in order to maintain your target heart rate. By using a target heart rate, you automatically compensate for your increased fitness, and you can maintain a good training effect.

One of the greatest advantages of heart rate monitoring is seen with older people. Many experts warn older adults not to exceed 90 percent of their maximum heart rate while exercising (9). They recommend that adults should work at between 70 and 90 percent of their maximum heart rate for effective yet safe training. Adults, then, should use the heart rate monitoring to prevent the activity from becoming too intense.

DURATION

The most violated principle of exercise is that of duration. The principle can be easily understood and is critical to the training effect you receive from any activity. Duration is inversely related to the intensity of the activity. The higher your jogging intensity, the shorter the duration can be. The lower your jogging intensity, the longer the duration should be. The absolute minimum duration is about fifteen minutes and is effective only if the exercise is fairly intense. No matter what the intensity, the effectiveness of the exercise increases as the duration increases. The best guidelines, according to the research, are as follows: jog at a heart rate greater than 70 percent of your maximum for 15 to 25 minutes per day. Jogging at this 70 percent heart rate, you should gradually increase the duration up to 25 minutes or so. Jogging at a heart rate of 80 to 85 percent, a duration of 15 to 20 minutes will do nicely. Research shows that 35 minutes is better than 25 minutes, and that 45 minutes is even better than 35 minutes per day. Increasing exercise durations up to about an hour a day will yield steadily increasing value; but beyond that point there are diminishing returns. Jogging durations of over one hour are probably not warranted in terms of physiological changes unless you are into competition (see Chapter 3 for information on competitive running).

FREQUENCY

The frequency of your exercise program is of utmost importance. Very little good will come from a sporadic or weekend type jogging program. Research indicates that four workouts per week are better than three, and that five are better than four. However, if you are unable to exercise daily, a similar training effect can be obtained from three workouts per week if you increase the duration of each workout by five or ten minutes. These sessions should be scheduled on alternate days. Two workouts per week are not effective for increasing cardiovascular fitness, even though they will maintain your desired level of fitness once you have reached it.

What advice would you give to a beginning jogger as to percent of maximum heart rate, duration, and frequency of exercise?

WARM-UP AND COOL DOWN

Each jogging period should be preceded by a warm-up and concluded with a cool-down period. These are important parts of your workout and will help you to jog safely and comfortably. Warming up will allow your body to make the numerous changes it needs to support the necessary increase in metabolic activity. It will also help stretch and loosen the tendons and ligaments so that injury will not easily occur.

As you warm-up, your heart will increase its rate and stroke volume gradually, thus increasing the amount of blood being pumped through the system. The blood vessels in your legs will open to allow this blood to flow past the cells, while the vessels in the abdominal region will close down to make more blood available to the muscles. At the same time, the lungs will begin to move more air in and out to supply oxygen to the increased volume of blood flowing through them. All of these changes occur in order to increase the amount of oxygen available to the muscle cells to support the great increase in oxidative activity which supplies energy for muscular contraction.

An interesting study was done which proves rather conclusively the need of warm-up. Forty-four normal men (ages twenty-one to fifty-two) were tested on two different occasions with and without a warm-up. All had normal electro-cardiographic (EKG) responses when they exercised after warming-up. However, during the second test session, when exercising without a warm-up, thirty-one of these men (70 percent) developed abnormal EKG changes (6). Apparently, the heart muscle also needs time to re-adjust the circulation so that enough oxygen is available during the jogging period.

Cooling down is as important as warming up. During aerobic exercise, the large muscles of the legs provide a real "boost" to the circulating blood and help it get back to the heart. Each time the leg muscles contract, blood is forced up the veins toward the heart. As the muscles relax, blood fills the veins but is not allowed to go back because of the valves in the veins. During work, the "muscle pump" (squeezing action of the legs) provides about half of the pumping action, while the heart provides the other half. Cooling down allows the muscle pump to continue to work until the total volume of blood being pumped is decreased to where the heart can handle it without help from the muscles.

An interesting true story illustrates the importance of cooling off. Several months ago, a well-trained faculty member was jogging across campus after a long run when suddenly the evening flag service began. Because of his respect for the flag, he stopped and stood at attention. Almost immediately, he passed out and fell to the ground from lack of blood being returned to the heart where it could be pumped to his head. If you are ever in such a situation, keep moving your legs while you stand to keep the muscle pump working.

It may surprise you to know that many problems with post-cardiac patients occur five to ten minutes *after* exercise when the entire load of blood must be pumped by the heart alone. These problems can be minimized by careful cooling-down procedures which allow the body systems to revert slowly to normal. Cooling-down slowly also helps the muscles rid themselves more effectively of the waste products of metabolism. Some studies have shown that less soreness occurs in subjects who cool down slowly, as compared to those who stop their exercise without a cool-down period.

Warming-up should include the preliminary stretching exercises discussed in chapter two, as well as a period of time where you jog slowly before increasing the tempo. Cooling-down can be easily accomplished by slowing down some distance before reaching your destination, finally coming to a walk. As you walk for the last few hundred yards, the body will re-adjust to the decreased need for oxygen, and you will have cooled down.

Persons who are not well informed often fail to realize the importance of a cool-down period. Can you give three reasons for gradually decreasing the intensity of exercise rather than decreasing abruptly?

MECHANICS OF JOGGING

There is no single correct way to jog since every one is not anatomically built exactly the same. There are, however, some general suggestions to follow which will reduce the chances for soreness and injury and thus make your jogging a more enjoyable experience.

Body   The best body position for jogging is to stand erect and keep the back as straight as is naturally comfortable. If a line were drawn from the ear to the ground, the back should be almost perpendicular to the ground while you are jogging. Bill Bowerman, former University of Oregon and U.S. Olympic Coach and one of the individuals credited with the introduction of the jogging concept to the United States, states that the pelvic position is the key to correct jogging posture. The pelvis should be tucked under or brought forward in relation to the rest of the body, as this assists in straightening the spine, which helps maintain an upright position of the body. This position should not be forced or uncomfortable but should be relaxed and effortless. The head should be held in a normal, erect position and the face, neck, and shoulder muscles should be relaxed.

Arms   Your arms should be relaxed and bent at the elbow so that the hand and elbow are approximately the same distance from the running surface. They should swing in rhythm with the movement of the legs and pass just above the hips and just slightly in front of the body. The hands should be aligned with the forearm and relaxed with the thumb slightly on the index finger. The position of the arms and hands should be relaxed without an excess of useless movement.

Feet   One of the most important factors in the mechanics of jogging is how your foot makes contact with the running surface. A common mistake made by many beginning joggers is to run on the toes. This practice will result in tight calf muscles and muscle soreness. The proper footplant technique is to land on the back one-third of the foot, then roll forward and lift from the front of the foot on your next stride. Another method that works quite well is to use a soft, relaxed flat-footed landing.

Stride   A common error is to over stride. This results in a waste of energy and contributes to body injury by throwing the body off-balance. The best method is to use a short stride that will allow the foot to contact the running surface beneath the knee instead of reaching the foot out in front of the body. Avoid excessive leg movements such as a high-knee lift or kick-up at the end of the stride, since both movements increase the effort of running and cause fatigue to occur more quickly.

To increase the efficiency of your jogging, listen for excessive noise when the feet contact the surface. Check to see if you rise or dip with your stride causing a bouncing effect, (sometimes the result of over-striding). Also check to see if you are leaning too far forward. Finally, check periodically to see if you have excessive arm and hand movement.

To improve running form indirectly, you should consider a flexibility and strength training program. By increasing your flexibility, you can now increase your stride length without placing an increase in stress on the body. It has been estimated that an increase in stride length of 4″ can take .5 seconds off the 100-yard dash time when stride frequency remains the same. If a person, through a flexibility program, increases the stride length, think what a great effect this would have on longer runs!

Strength training can improve running efficiency in a variety of ways. An increase in upper body strength can help to combat the onset of fatigue that causes many people to adopt a poor running form. As indicated before, the arms are an important factor in running. Increased strength in your arms and upper body can contribute to movement of the body, even as the legs begin to tire.

Increased strength of the lower body is important, as the act of jogging may not provide enough of a stimulus to cause strength gains. Also, in order to maintain a balance of strength in the various muscle groups, strength training is advised.

With a little practice, you will develop a style of running that is relaxed and will enable you to cover the greatest distance with the least amount of effort.

FLEXIBILITY

Dr. George Sheehan, the medical advisor for *Runner's World* has said, "When you run, three things happen to your body, and two of them are bad."

The good thing is that the body gets better at running. The two bad things are (1) the muscles on the back of your body become strong and lose flexibility and (2) the front muscles don't. The situation causes an imbalance which can lead to injury.

Flexibility exercises can't solve all of the injury problems experienced by joggers, but they can help.

Flexibility refers to the range of motion at a joint or a series of joints. Since movement is accomplished by the shortening and lengthening of muscle tissue, tight ligaments, muscles, and connective tissue can limit the range of motion or flexibility and thus restrict movement.

The type of stretching movement used in a flexibility exercise is very important since there are receptors, located in the muscles and joints which are stimulated by fast, jerky, bouncy movements. When these receptors are stimulated, the muscle you are attempting to stretch contracts and resists the stretching motion. This reduces the effectiveness of your stretching and often causes muscle soreness.

These receptors are not, however, stimulated by slow, sustained stretching. Thus, the muscles can relax and lengthen and so increased flexibility can occur. Much muscle soreness is prevented or alleviated by this type of movement.

Some guidelines to use in your flexibility program follow.

1. You must have a daily stretching program because it takes time to make progress in flexibility.
2. Select simple exercises to begin stretching a muscle group.
3. Be sure to warm up the muscles gradually before doing any stretching exercises.
4. Move into the stretching position slowly and continue until stretch on the muscle is felt. Remember that excessive pain is not part of a good stretching program.
5. After reaching a good stretch position, hold that position for five or more seconds.
6. As the muscles are being stretched, always try to relax the muscle that is being placed in a stretching position.
7. When the stretching exercise is complete, release the body slowly from the exercise position.
8. It is important to remember that stretching exercises are not meant to be competitive. When you try too hard, it can lead to injury and a loss in flexibility.

Some of the following stretching exercises should be performed each day before jogging (3) (see Figures 2–4 to 2–11). It may seem like a time-consuming effort, but proper stretching will reduce the possibility of muscle and joint injury.

Uninformed joggers sometimes try to increase flexibility by quick bouncing or swinging movements. Can you explain why this approach is physiologically unsound?

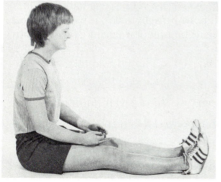 

Muscles stretched: Hamstrings.
Starting position: Sit on the floor with the legs straight and together.
Action: Extend the arms forward toward the toes, palms up. Stretch to or beyond

the toes until stretch pain is felt. Hold 3–5 seconds. Return to starting position.
Precautions: Do not bob. Keep the knees straight.
Repetitions: 5.

FIGURE 2–4 Sitting toe-touch.

From *Fitness for Life—An Individualized Approach,* by P. E. Allsen, J. Harrison, and B. Vance, 1976. Reprinted by permission of the publisher, Wm. C. Brown Publishers, Dubuque, Iowa 52001

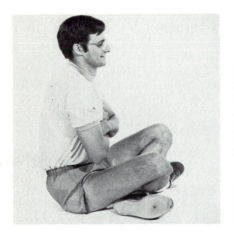

Muscles stretched: **Back extensors.**
Starting position: Sit with the legs crossed and arms folded or relaxed.
Action: Tuck the chin and curl forward attempting to touch the forehead to the knees. Hold 3–5 seconds. Return to starting position.
Precautions: Do not bob. Keep the hips on the mat.
Repetitions: 5.

FIGURE 2–5 Indian curl.

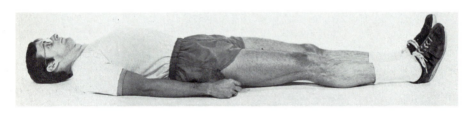

Muscles stretched: **Low back extensors.**
Starting position: Lie on back.
Action: Bring both knees to the chest, grabbing just under the knees and pulling the knees toward the armpits. Hold 5 seconds. Return to starting position.
Precautions: Avoid pulling with the knees together.
Repetitions: 5.

FIGURE 2–6 Knee-chest curl.

From *Fitness for Life—An Individualized Approach,* by P. E. Allsen, J. Harrison, and B. Vance, 1976. Reprinted by permission of the publisher, Wm. C. Brown Publishers, Dubuque, Iowa 52001

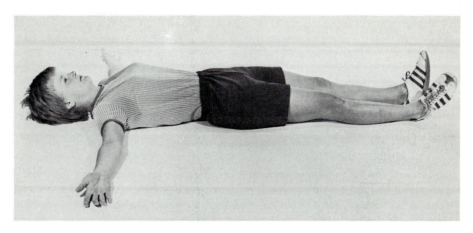

Muscles stretched: **Trunk rotators.**
Starting position: Lie on the back with the arms extended to the side at shoulder level.
Action: Raise the left leg to a vertical position, keeping the leg straight. Twist the body to touch the left leg to the **right hand. Hold 3–5 seconds. Return to** starting position. Repeat to opposite side.
Precautions: Keep the knees straight. Keep the arms and trunk on the mat.
Repetitions: 5 to each side.

FIGURE 2–7 Leg-over.

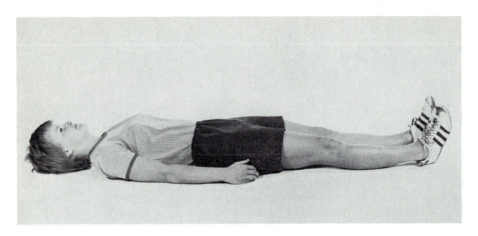

Muscles stretched: **Hip flexors.**
Starting position: Lie on the back with
the legs extended.
Action: Bring the left knee to the chest,
grabbing just under the knee with both
hands. Pull until a stretch pain is felt.

Hold 3–5 seconds. Return to starting
position. Repeat to opposite side.
Precautions: Keep the extended leg
straight and on the floor. Stretch slowly.
Repetitions: 5 to each side.

FIGURE 2–8 Lying knee-pull.

From *Fitness for Life—An Individualized Approach,* by P. E. Allsen, J. Harrison, and B. Vance,
1976. Reprinted by permission of the publisher, Wm. C. Brown Publishers, Dubuque, Iowa 52001

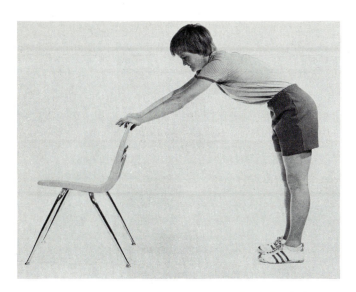

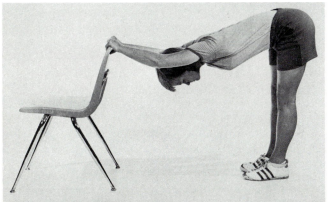

Muscles stretched: **Pectoral muscles.**
Starting position: Stand with feet apart (sideways) facing the back of the chair. Reach forward and place both hands on the chair back.
Action: Draw the head and chest downward by contracting the abdominal muscles. Hold 3–5 seconds. Return to starting position.
Precautions: Keep the feet spread and well back from the chair. Keep the lower back flat with no arch.
Repetitions: 5.

FIGURE 2–9 Chair stretch.

Muscles Stretched: **Heel cord,** gastrocnemius, soleus.
Starting position: Stand facing the wall with the palms against the wall and the body at arm's length. Spread the feet apart slightly.
Action: Keeping the feet flat and the body in a straight line, lean forward allowing the elbows to bend slightly until a stretch pain is felt in the calf muscles. Hold 3–5 seconds. Return to starting position.
Precautions: Keep the knees and body straight and the feet flat. For more stretch, put a book under the balls of the feet.
Repetitions: 5.

FIGURE 2–10 Heel-cord stretch.

From *Fitness for Life—An Individualized Approach,* by P. E. Allsen, J. Harrison, and B. Vance, 1976. Reprinted by permission of the publisher, Wm. C. Brown Publishers, Dubuque, Iowa 52001

Muscles stretched: **Muscles and** ligaments of the pelvic girdle.
Starting position: Stand with feet together and right side to wall, about 18 inches from the wall. Place right hand and forearm against the wall at shoulder level. Place the heel of the left hand on the buttocks.
Action: Keeping the body straight and facing forward, move the hips forward and inward to the wall below the hand by contracting the abdominal and gluteal (buttock) muscles and pushing with the left hand. Return to starting position. Repeat to opposite side.
Precautions: Keep the knees straight. Keep the hips and shoulders facing forward.
Repetitions: 3 to each side.

FIGURE 2–11 Billig stretch.

From *Fitness for Life—An Individualized Approach,* by P. E. Allsen, J. Harrison, and B. Vance, 1976. Reprinted by permission of the publisher, Wm. C. Brown Publishers, Dubuque, Iowa 52001

HOW TO BEGIN

Now that you have learned the basic principles which you can use to make your jogging program effective, it is important to know how to begin your program so that you will not become discouraged and quit before the training effect begins to take place. Most people who begin a jogging program have been inactive for some time but expect to become conditioned in a very short time. They nearly always try to do too much too soon. You must fight the impulse to jog too intensely or for too long a time at the beginning.

The 16 week program (Table 2–1) that follows is based on a suggested daily duration of continuous activity. Depending upon your initial fitness level, you can either start with walking, a walk-jog, or continuous jogging for that duration. Each person has to determine his or her starting point and standards of progress. The goal is to work up to at least 30 minutes a day at a comfortable pace. Remember, these are only suggested guidelines, and as you become conditioned, you may wish to exercise longer on any given day. As you progress through the program, you will be able to increase your cardiovascular fitness and jog with ease.

If you are beginning your exercise program at an extremely low level of fitness and have not been active for some time, it would be a good idea to ignore the intensity principle for the first two weeks and begin by walking for the suggested duration. Do not take either fitness test described in chapter 1 until you have toughened your body by the walking program.

If you have been fairly active, you should take the Sharkey's Test of fitness to determine your initial fitness rating. If you are jogging regularly for more than 15 minutes, you should take the Coopers 1.5 mile run to determine an initial fitness category. If you score in the poor or very poor category with either test, you should spend the first two weeks walking briskly for the recommended times. If you score in the fair to good category, it would still be a good idea to walk for several days before beginning to jog. After several days of walking, you may feel good enough to jog slowly for short periods during your walk. This is acceptable. However, do not try to jog the entire duration for at least two weeks. After this time, you will find that your jogging periods will automatically increase and that your walking periods will not have to be as long in order for recovery to take place.

When you feel strong enough to run for 3 or 4 minutes at a time, you can begin to check your pulse for proper intensity. Remember to maintain about 70 percent of your maximum heart rate for the first month or so. After you can jog for the entire duration, you can begin to increase the intensity slowly to the 80 to 85 percent level. *Do not be in a hurry to increase the intensity.* You should be able to carry on a fairly normal conversation while you jog. If you are working too hard to talk, slow down.

If you scored in the very good, excellent, or superior range, you can begin jogging in conformity with the heart rate guidelines previously discussed. You may feel more comfortable using the 70 percent level for the first two weeks, then moving up to the 80 percent range at that time. Your own body is the best indicator of what is best for you, so let it tell you how rapidly to progress. If anything, most people try to do too much too soon.

TABLE 2–1 SIXTEEN-WEEK JOGGING PROGRAM

	Week 1		Week 2		Week 3
M	20 min	M	25 min	M	30 min
T	20 min	T	25 min	T	25 min
W	25 min	W	30 min	W	35 min
Th	20 min	Th	25 min	Th	30 min
F	20 min	F	27 min	F	25 min
S	27 min	S	30 min	S	35 min
Weekly Average	22 min		26 min		30 min
	Week 4		**Week 5**		**Week 6**
M	30 min	M	30 min	M	35 min
T	30 min	T	30 min	T	20 min
W	25 min	W	30 min	W	40 min
Th	35 min	Th	30 min	Th	30 min
F	30 min	F	30 min	F	25 min
S	30 min	S	30 min	S	30 min
Weekly Average	30 min		30 min		30 min
	Week 7		**Week 8**		**Week 9**
M	35 min	M	40 min	M	30 min
T	20 min	T	25 min	T	25 min
W	40 min	W	30 min	W	35 min
Th	30 min	Th	Rest	Th	30 min
F	25 min	F	40 min	F	25 min
S	30 min	S	45 min	S	35 min
Weekly Average	30 min		30 min		30 min
	Week 10		**Week 11**		**Week 12**
M	40 min	M	30 min	M	35 min
T	25 min	T	25 min	T	35 min
W	30 min	W	35 min	W	35 min
Th	Rest	Th	20 min	Th	35 min
F	40 min	F	25 min	F	35 min
S	45 min	S	35 min	S	35 min
Weekly Average	30 min		35 min		35 min

	Week 13		Week 14		Week 15		Week 16
M	35 min	M	60 min	M	60 min	M	90 min
T	35 min	T	Rest	T	Rest	T	Rest
W	35 min	W	60 min	W	60 min	W	30 min
Th	Rest	Th	Rest	Th	Rest	Th	60 min
F	55 min	F	60 min	F	60 min	F	Rest
S	50 min	S	30 min	S	30 min	S	60 min
Weekly Average	35 min		35 min		35 min		40 min

Figure 2–12 shows how you should use the information you have learned for a typical jogging workout. Remember that you should always warm up before the jog by first stretching and then jogging easily and slowly. Allow the heart rate to move slowly up to your target heart rate, then maintain it for the entire duration of the exercise.

You may wish to use the technique called interval training. Figure 2–13 shows how this technique can be used effectively. Starting with a warm-up period, jog for several minutes at your 70 percent target heart rate, and then increase the intensity for 30 seconds or a minute to the 80 to 90 percent level. Return to a slow jog until the heart rate reaches 70 percent again, and repeat the sequence. This procedure can be repeated for the entire duration of your workout. This is similar to the technique you will use when you first begin your program, except that the intensity will be higher than the initial intensities.

Remember to cool down following each workout by slowing your pace for a minute or two and then walking for several minutes, to allow your blood flow to decrease before you shut off the muscle pump.

The 16-week jogging program (Table 2–1) was included as a guide to the proper duration. However, don't feel restricted by these guidelines. You may wish to run for a longer period from time to time as you become more trained. This type of activity is encouraged. The real joy of jogging occurs as you break away from the restrictions of the track or field and enjoy the changing panorama of running a country road or by a stream or river. Just be sure that you slow down and decrease the intensity when you increase the duration. Remember, you want your fitness program to be fun. The best way to keep it fun is to "train, not strain." Jogging should not cause complete fatigue at any stage. Arthur Lydiard, the outstanding coach from New Zealand, said that one should never go beyond the stage of "pleasant tiredness." You should be able to carry on a conversation as you jog, especially if you increase the duration over the guidelines as presented in Table 2–1.

The terrain over which you run is an important factor in your jogging program. What advantages and disadvantages can you think of in choosing to run around city blocks, on a track, or in open country? Which surface is safest? Which is most challenging? Which places most stress on muscles and joints?

RECORDING PROGRESS

Table 2–2 has been included to help you evaluate your progress as you begin your jogging program. The first two weeks should be used for walking and easy intervals of jogging, with no intensity requirements. This is the time you should use to toughen the muscle-skeletal system and learn the heart rate monitoring techniques. At the end of two weeks, if you feel good and have no problems with your legs or feet, you may begin to monitor your pulse rate at the 70 percent level. If you are over 35 or extremely overweight, you may wish to extend this initial toughening phase for one or two weeks longer. Don't feel hurried during this phase.

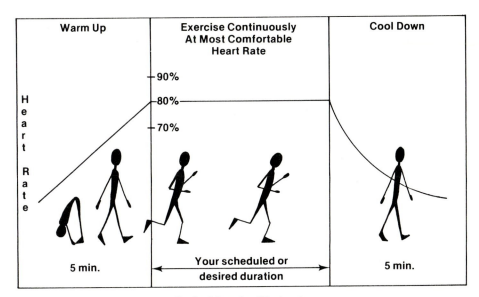

Typical Jogging Workout

FIGURE 2–12 Typical jogging workout.

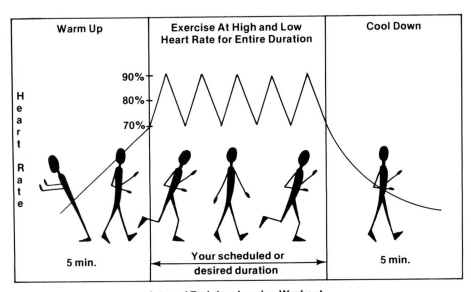

Interval Training Jogging Workout

FIGURE 2–13 Interval training jogging
workout.

TABLE 2–2   16-WEEK PROGRESS CHART

		Suggested Time	Actual Time	Dist.	Average Heart Rate	How I Felt
M	Week 1	20				
T		20				
W		25				
T		20				
F		20				
S		27				
M	Week 2	25				
T		25				
W		30				
T		25				
F		27				
S		30				
M	Week 3	30				
T		25				
W		35				
T		30				
F		25				
S		35				
M	Week 4	30				
T		30				
W		25				
T		35				
F		30				
S		30				
M	Week 5	30				
T		30				
W		30				
T		30				
F		30				
S		30				
M	Week 6	35				
T		20				
W		40				
T		30				
F		25				
S		30				
M	Week 7	35				
T		20				
W		40				
T		30				
F		25				
S		30				

TABLE 2–2—CONTINUED

		Suggested Time	Actual Time	Dist.	Average Heart Rate	How I Felt
M		40				
T		25				
W	Week 8	30				
T		Rest				
F		40				
S		45				
M		30				
T		25				
W	Week 9	35				
T		30				
F		25				
S		35				
M		40				
T		25				
W	Week 10	30				
T		Rest				
F		40				
S		45				
M		30				
T		25				
W	Week 11	35				
T		20				
F		25				
S		35				
M		35				
T		35				
W	Week 12	35				
T		35				
F		35				
S		35				
M		35				
T		35				
W	Week 13	35				
T		Rest				
F		55				
S		50				
M		60				
T		Rest				
W	Week 14	60				
T		Rest				
F		60				
S		30				

TABLE 2-2—CONTINUED

		Suggested Time	Actual Time	Dist.	Average Heart Rate	How I Felt
M		60				
T	Week 15	Rest				
W		60				
T		Rest				
F		60				
S		30				
M		90				
T	Week 16	Rest				
W		30				
T		60				
F		Rest				
S		60				

Once you have begun to monitor your heart rate at the 70 percent level, record both heart rate and duration in the appropriate blanks. Remember, increase the duration 5 to 10 minutes if you are jogging three times a week. Separate tearout sheets are in the back of the book for future use.

ANAEROBIC THRESHOLD

As mentioned before, our body is basically an aerobic machine—it needs oxygen to produce energy for muscular contraction. However, we are also able to produce a small amount of energy for a short period of time *anaerobically* (without oxygen). This anaerobic source of energy is really important for those times when we must move, but are unable to breathe. For instance, this source of energy allows us to swim underwater for a short period of time, or to run from a burning building while holding our breath. Using energy from this system is like borrowing money from a bank; you are limited in the amount you can borrow and it must be paid back after the loan.

Normal daily activities depend primarily upon the aerobic energy systems and do not involve the anaerobic mechanisms to any great extent. However, at higher work loads, there is a point where the aerobic systems are unable to supply enough energy to support the bigger work level, and anaerobic energy must be produced to help out. This point is called the "anaerobic threshold."

Everyone has an anaerobic threshold. This threshold represents a "limit" to continuous work for each person. If you jog at or below your anaerobic threshold, you are able to run for long distances because the energy at this intensity can be supplied aerobically and no energy debt occurs. However, if you run even a little bit faster, the anaerobic systems begin to supply energy, and you experience fatigue after a period of time, depending on how far above the threshold you are working.

As you train, your anaerobic threshold will rise, and you will be able to work at a higher relative work level without fatigue. This is why trained joggers enjoy working at from 80–85 percent of their maximum heart rate while beginners usually work at slightly lower levels. Training also increases your total aerobic capacity. With the increase in aerobic capacity and the rise in anaerobic threshold, you will soon be able to jog faster and for a longer period of time than you even thought possible.

What is meant by the term "anaerobic threshold"?

3 *Jogging and Weight Control*

Obesity is a major health hazard. In the publication "Health Implications of Obesity" (National Institute of Health Consensus Development Conference Statement—1985), a group of experts stated that obesity "was clearly associated with hypertension, hypercholesterolemia (high blood cholesterol), NIDDM (adult onset diabetes), and with increased incidence of certain cancers and other medical problems. They stated that thirty-four million adult Americans are at least 20 percent above "desirable" weight, and that this level constitutes an established health hazard.

The typical approach to this problem is the "fad" diet. Various types of diets are published routinely in popular magazines and include such names as the Hollywood diet, the California diet, the Grapefruit diet, and the Drinking Man's diet. Some rely on one specific food (such as grapefruit) for total nutrition, others require an avoidance of carbohydrates, and others sell a liquid protein or some "special" Chinese herb. Most violate the basic principles of good nutrition and in many cases are more dangerous to health than is obesity.

Another approach is the "diet clinic." These clinics are often run by unscrupulous men or women who have no background in nutrition or weight control and who bilk the population out of millions of dollars each year.

Despite the great interest in diets and the millions spent each year in weight loss programs, 60 percent of all Americans are overweight by age 50.

The important factor is not how much you weigh, but how much of the body weight is fat. "Normal" fat levels for men range from 15 to 25 percent; for women, from 20 to 30 percent. Obesity is usually defined as anything over 25% fat in men and 30% fat in women. Most male distance runners have less than 6 percent fat and female runners usually have around 10–12 percent.

These levels are probably out of reach for the average person, but joggers will surely get thinner if they follow the guidelines in this section.

We have included two formulae to help you estimate your percent fat. The formula for women requires a measurement from the hips and waist and height in inches. Measure the hips at the *largest* circumference and the waist at the umbilical (belly button) using a standard tape measure. (See Figures 3–1 and 3–2.) Measure each circumference several times and record the average of the closest measurements. Throw out any that seem too far out.

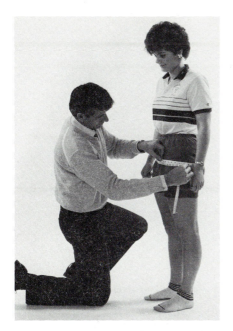

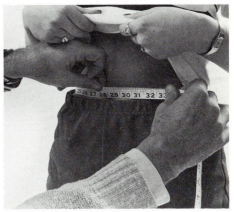

FIGURE 3–1 Measure the hips at the largest circumference several times, and use the average of the closest measurement in table 3–1.

FIGURE 3–2 Measure the waist at the umbilicus (belly button).

Now enter Table 3–1 with the measurements and write down the "constant" number associated with each. Percent fat is calculated by adding the "constant" number associated with the hips measurement to the "constant" number from the waist measurement and then subtracting the "constant" number for the height.

For example: If you are 64″ tall and your hip measurements are 40 inches and your waist 26 inches, what is your percent fat?

The constant number for 40″ hip measurement is	<u>47.44</u>
The index number for 26″ waist measurement is	<u>18.49</u>
Added together	<u>65.93</u>
Now subtract the constant number for height	<u>39.01</u>
The result is <u>percent fat</u>	<u>26.92</u>
Your constant number for hip measurement is	_____
Your index number for waist measurement is	_____
Added together	_____
Now subtract your constant number for height	_____
The result is <u>your percent fat</u>	_____

TABLE 3–1 CONVERSION CONSTANTS TO PREDICT PERCENT BODY FAT (WOMEN)

| | Hips | | Abdomen | | Height |
In.	Constant A	In.	Constant B	In.	Constant C
30	33.48	20	14.22	55	33.52
31	34.87	21	14.93	56	34.13
32	36.27	22	15.64	57	34.74
33	37.67	23	16.35	58	35.35
34	39.06	24	17.06	59	35.96
35	40.46	25	17.78	60	36.57
36	41.86	26	18.49	61	37.18
37	43.25	27	19.20	62	37.79
38	44.65	28	19.91	63	38.40
39	46.05	29	20.62	64	39.01
40	47.44	30	21.33	65	39.62
41	48.84	31	22.04	66	40.23
42	50.24	32	22.75	67	40.84
43	51.64	33	23.46	68	41.45
44	53.03	34	24.18	69	42.06
45	54.43	35	24.89	70	42.67
46	55.83	36	25.60	71	43.28
47	57.22	37	26.31	72	43.89
48	58.62	38	27.02	73	44.50
49	60.02	39	27.73	74	45.11
50	61.42	40	28.44	75	45.72
51	62.81	41	29.15	76	46.32
52	64.21	42	29.87	77	46.93
53	65.61	43	30.58	78	47.54
54	67.00	44	31.29	79	48.15
55	68.40	45	32.00	80	48.76
56	69.80	46	32.71	81	49.37
57	71.19	47	33.42	82	49.98
58	72.59	48	34.13	83	50.59
59	73.99	49	34.84	84	51.20
60	75.39	50	35.56	85	51.81

Regression equation for this table courtesy of Captain Richard W. Coté III (USAF Academy) and Jack H. Wilmore (University of Arizona).
From Remmington, Fisher, and Parent. *How to Lower Your Fat Thermostat.* Vitality House International, 1983.

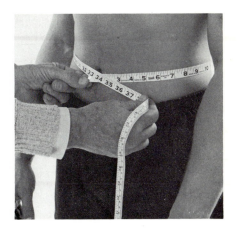

FIGURE 3–3 Measure the wrist just in front at the bones where it bends. Subtract this value from your waist measurement to determine percent fat from table 3–2.

FIGURE 3–4 Measure the waist at the umbilicus (belly button).

Men simply measure the wrist just in front at the bones where the wrist bends and subtract this value from the circumference of the waist at the umbilical (belly button). (See Figures 3–3 and 3–4.) Then enter Table 3–2 (see pp. 42–43) with this number and your body weight in pounds to get percent fat.

For example, if you weigh 185 pounds, your waist is 36 inches, and your wrist measurement is 7.5 inches, you subtract 7.5 from 36 to get 28.5. Use this number to find the proper column and go down that column to 185 (your body weight). The percent fat is 18. An example of how this calculation would look follows:

The waist measurement is	36
The wrist measurement is	7.5
The difference is	28.5
At a body weight of	185
The percent fat is	18

Now, calculate your percent fat from the table.

Your waist measurement is _____

Your wrist measurement is _____

The difference is _____

Now, enter the table with your weight _____

The result is your percent fat _____

TABLE 3–2   WAIST MINUS WRIST (INCHES)

Wt. (Lbs.)	22	22.5	23	23.5	24	24.5	25	25.5	26	26.5	27	27.5	28	28.5	29	29.5	30	30.5	31	31.5	32	32.5	33	33.5	34	34.5	35	35.5	36
120	4	6	8	10	12	14	16	18	20	21	23	25	27	29	31	33	35	37	39	41	43	45	47	49	50	52	54	56	58
125	4	6	7	9	11	13	15	17	19	20	22	24	26	28	30	32	33	35	37	39	41	43	45	46	48	50	52	54	56
130	3	5	7	9	11	12	14	16	18	20	21	23	25	27	28	30	32	34	36	37	39	41	43	44	46	48	50	52	53
135	3	5	7	8	10	12	13	15	17	19	20	22	24	26	27	29	31	32	34	36	38	39	41	43	44	46	48	50	51
140	3	5	6	8	10	11	13	15	16	18	19	21	23	24	26	28	29	31	33	34	36	38	39	41	43	44	46	48	49
145	3	4	6	7	9	11	12	14	15	17	19	20	22	23	25	27	28	30	31	33	35	36	38	39	41	43	44	46	47
150	2	4	6	7	9	10	12	13	15	16	18	19	21	23	24	26	27	29	30	32	33	35	36	38	40	41	43	44	46
155	2	4	5	7	8	10	11	13	14	16	17	19	20	22	23	25	26	28	29	31	32	34	35	37	38	40	41	43	44
160	2	4	5	6	8	9	11	12	14	15	17	18	19	21	22	24	25	27	28	30	31	33	34	35	37	38	40	41	43
165	2	3	5	6	8	9	10	12	13	15	16	17	19	20	22	23	24	26	27	29	30	31	33	34	36	37	38	40	41
170	2	3	4	6	7	9	10	11	13	14	15	17	18	19	21	22	24	25	26	28	29	30	32	33	34	36	37	39	40
175	2	3	4	6	7	8	10	11	12	13	15	16	17	19	20	21	23	24	25	27	28	29	31	32	33	35	36	37	39
180	1	3	4	5	7	8	9	10	12	13	14	16	17	18	19	21	22	23	25	26	27	28	30	31	32	34	35	36	37
185	1	3	4	5	6	8	9	10	11	13	14	15	16	18	19	20	21	23	24	25	26	28	29	30	31	33	34	35	36
190	1	2	4	5	6	7	8	10	11	12	13	15	16	17	18	19	21	22	23	24	26	27	28	29	30	32	33	34	35
195	1	2	3	5	6	7	8	9	11	12	13	14	15	16	18	19	20	21	22	24	25	26	27	28	30	31	32	33	34
200	1	2	3	4	6	7	8	9	10	11	12	14	15	16	17	18	19	21	22	23	24	25	26	28	29	30	31	32	33
205	1	2	3	4	5	6	8	9	10	11	12	13	14	15	17	18	19	20	21	22	23	25	26	27	28	29	30	31	32
210	1	2	3	4	5	6	7	8	9	11	12	13	14	15	16	17	18	19	21	22	23	24	25	26	27	28	29	30	32
215	1	2	3	4	5	6	7	8	9	10	11	12	13	15	16	17	18	19	20	21	22	23	24	25	26	28	29	30	31
220	0	2	3	4	5	6	7	8	9	10	11	12	13	14	15	16	17	18	19	20	22	23	24	25	26	27	28	29	30
225	0	1	2	3	4	6	7	8	9	10	11	12	13	14	15	16	17	18	19	20	21	22	23	24	25	26	27	28	29
230	0	1	2	3	4	5	6	7	8	9	10	11	12	13	14	15	16	17	18	19	20	21	22	23	24	25	26	27	28
235	0	1	2	3	4	5	6	7	8	9	10	11	12	13	14	15	16	17	18	19	20	21	22	23	24	25	26	27	28
240	0	1	2	3	4	5	6	7	8	9	10	11	12	13	14	15	16	17	17	18	19	20	21	22	23	24	25	26	27
245	0	1	2	3	4	5	6	7	8	9	9	10	11	12	13	14	15	16	17	18	19	20	21	22	23	24	25	26	27
250	0	1	2	3	4	5	6	6	7	8	9	10	11	12	13	14	15	16	17	18	18	19	20	21	22	23	24	25	26
255	0	1	2	3	3	4	5	6	7	8	9	10	11	12	13	14	14	15	16	17	18	19	20	21	22	23	24	24	25
260	0	1	2	2	3	4	5	6	7	8	9	10	10	11	12	13	14	15	16	17	18	19	19	20	21	22	23	24	25
265	0	1	1	2	3	4	5	6	7	8	8	9	10	11	12	13	14	15	15	16	17	18	19	20	21	22	22	23	24
270	0	1	1	2	3	4	5	6	7	7	8	9	10	11	12	13	13	14	15	16	17	18	19	19	20	21	22	23	24
275	0	0	1	2	3	4	5	5	6	7	8	9	10	11	11	12	13	14	15	16	16	17	18	19	20	21	22	22	23
280	0	0	1	2	3	4	4	5	6	7	8	9	9	10	11	12	13	14	14	15	16	17	18	19	19	20	21	22	23
285	0	0	1	2	3	4	4	5	6	7	8	8	9	10	11	12	12	13	14	15	16	17	17	18	19	20	21	21	22
290	0	0	1	2	3	3	4	5	6	7	7	8	9	10	11	11	12	13	14	15	15	16	17	18	19	19	20	21	22
295	0	0	1	2	2	3	4	5	6	6	7	8	9	10	10	11	12	13	14	14	15	16	17	17	18	19	20	21	21
300	0	0	1	2	2	3	4	5	5	6	7	8	9	9	10	11	12	12	13	14	15	16	16	17	18	19	19	20	21

Penrose, Nelson and Fisher. "Generalized Body Composition Prediction Equation for Men Using Simple Measurement Techniques," *Medicine and Science in Sports and Exercise,* Vol. 17, No. 2, April, 1985.

TABLE 3-2—CONTINUED

Wt. (Lbs.)	36.5	37	37.5	38	38.5	39	39.5	40	40.5	41	41.5	42	42.5	43	43.5	44	44.5	45	45.5	46	46.5	47	47.5	48	48.5	49	49.5	50
120	60	62	64	66	68	70	72	74	76	77	79	81	83	85	87	89	91	93	95	97	99	99	99	99	99	99	99	99
125	58	59	61	63	65	67	69	71	72	74	76	78	80	82	84	85	87	89	91	93	95	96	98	99	99	99	99	99
130	55	57	59	61	62	64	66	68	69	71	73	75	77	78	80	82	84	86	87	89	91	93	94	96	98	99	99	99
135	53	55	56	58	60	62	63	65	67	68	70	72	74	75	77	79	80	82	84	86	87	89	91	92	94	96	98	99
140	51	53	54	56	58	59	61	63	64	66	68	69	71	72	74	76	77	79	81	82	84	86	87	89	91	92	94	96
145	49	51	52	54	55	57	59	60	62	63	65	67	68	70	71	73	75	76	78	79	81	83	84	86	87	89	91	92
150	47	49	50	52	53	55	57	58	60	61	63	64	66	67	69	70	72	74	75	77	78	80	81	83	84	86	87	89
155	46	47	49	50	52	53	55	56	58	59	61	62	64	65	67	68	70	71	73	74	76	77	79	80	82	83	85	86
160	44	46	47	48	50	51	53	54	56	57	59	60	61	63	64	66	67	69	70	72	73	75	76	77	79	80	82	83
165	43	44	45	47	48	50	51	52	54	55	57	58	60	61	62	64	65	67	68	69	71	72	74	75	76	78	79	81
170	41	43	44	45	47	48	49	51	52	54	55	56	58	59	60	62	63	64	66	67	69	70	71	73	74	75	77	78
175	40	41	43	44	45	47	48	49	51	52	53	55	56	57	59	60	61	63	64	65	66	68	69	70	72	73	74	76
180	39	40	41	43	44	45	47	48	49	50	52	53	54	56	57	58	59	61	62	63	65	66	67	68	70	71	72	74
185	38	39	40	41	43	44	45	46	48	49	50	51	53	54	55	56	58	59	60	61	63	64	65	66	68	69	70	71
190	37	38	39	40	41	43	44	45	46	48	49	50	51	52	54	55	56	57	58	60	61	62	63	65	66	67	68	69
195	35	37	38	39	40	41	43	44	45	46	47	49	50	51	52	53	55	56	57	58	59	60	62	63	64	65	66	68
200	35	36	37	38	39	40	41	43	44	45	46	47	48	50	51	52	53	54	55	57	58	59	60	61	62	63	65	66
205	34	35	36	37	38	39	40	41	43	44	45	46	47	48	49	51	52	53	54	55	56	57	58	60	61	62	63	64
210	33	34	35	36	37	38	39	40	42	43	44	45	46	47	48	49	50	51	53	54	55	56	57	58	59	60	61	62
215	32	33	34	35	36	37	38	39	40	42	43	44	45	46	47	48	49	50	51	52	53	54	56	57	58	59	60	61
220	31	32	33	34	35	36	37	38	39	41	42	43	44	45	46	47	48	49	50	51	52	53	54	55	56	57	58	59
225	30	31	32	33	34	35	36	37	38	40	41	42	43	44	45	46	47	48	49	50	51	52	53	54	55	56	57	58
230	30	31	32	33	34	35	36	37	38	39	40	41	42	43	44	45	46	47	48	49	50	51	52	53	54	55	56	57
235	29	30	31	32	33	34	35	36	37	38	39	40	41	42	43	44	45	46	47	48	49	50	51	51	52	53	54	55
240	28	29	30	31	32	33	34	35	36	37	38	39	40	41	42	43	44	45	46	46	47	48	49	50	51	52	53	54
245	27	28	29	30	31	32	33	34	35	36	37	38	39	40	41	42	43	44	44	45	46	47	48	49	50	51	52	53
250	27	28	29	30	31	31	32	33	34	35	36	37	38	39	40	41	42	43	44	44	45	46	47	48	49	50	51	52
255	26	27	28	29	30	31	32	33	34	34	35	36	37	38	39	40	41	42	43	44	44	45	46	47	48	49	50	51
260	26	27	27	28	29	30	31	32	33	34	35	35	36	37	38	39	40	41	42	43	43	44	45	46	47	48	49	50
265	25	26	27	28	29	29	30	31	32	33	34	35	36	36	37	38	39	40	41	42	43	43	44	45	46	47	48	49
270	25	25	26	27	28	29	30	31	31	32	33	34	35	36	37	37	38	39	40	41	42	43	43	44	45	46	47	48
275	24	25	26	27	27	28	29	30	31	32	32	33	34	35	36	37	38	38	39	40	41	42	43	43	44	45	46	47
280	24	24	25	26	27	28	29	29	30	31	32	33	33	34	35	36	37	38	38	39	40	41	42	43	43	44	45	46
285	23	24	25	26	26	27	28	29	30	30	31	32	33	34	34	35	36	37	38	39	39	40	41	42	43	43	44	45
290	23	23	24	25	26	27	27	28	29	30	31	31	32	33	34	35	35	36	37	38	39	39	40	41	42	43	43	44
295	22	23	24	25	25	26	27	28	28	29	30	31	32	32	33	34	35	36	36	37	38	39	39	40	41	42	43	43
300	22	22	23	24	25	26	26	27	28	29	29	30	31	32	33	33	34	35	36	36	37	38	39	39	40	41	42	43

LOSING WEIGHT

In the past, scientists have taught that weight control was simply a matter of energy balance and that you were fat because you "over-ate." Of course, the solution seemed simple, "Just cut down on the amount of food you eat and you'll lose your extra weight." The trouble is, no one loses weight by "cutting down on food." Surveys indicate that about 56 percent of the population is on a diet at any given time and estimates from clinics, studies, and obesity specialists indicate that only about 5% of all dieters are successful and that the other 95% either fail to lose weight, or regain any pounds they lose within a fairly short time. The failure of diets is probably the reason there are so many diets on the market and why almost every woman's magazine runs a new diet every month.

Recent research gives insight into the reason diets fail so often. Apparently, each of us has a "weight regulating mechanism" or "fat thermostat" in the brain that works just like the thermostat in your house. If your house begins to get cold, the thermostat turns on the furnace to keep the temperature comfortable. In a similar way, when you restrict the intake of food (as in dieting), the fat thermostat turns down *your* heat so you don't use so many calories. After a few weeks, your body adjusts to the lower intake of your diet and you hit the well-known weight-loss plateau. For example, if you are eating 1500 calories a day and decide to lose some weight, you may decrease your intake to 1000 calories. The metabolic rate will soon begin to fall and by 3 weeks you will begin to live comfortably on 1000 calories and further weight loss will stop. Then, after you get discouraged and begin to eat 1500 calories again, your weight will rise to the old weight and may even go higher.

Studies show that the more you go through this weight loss-weight gain cycle, the more slowly you lose weight and the more quickly you regain it.

How do you lose weight if dieting doesn't work? This is where jogging comes in.

There are several important reasons why jogging can have a major effect on weight loss and not for the reasons you may have thought:

1. The first reason to jog (or exercise in any similar way) is to *reset* the fat thermostat to a lower level. Exercise is always associated with leanness. Animals in the wild are lean; in cages they may get fat. Even lean world-class runners get fatter in the off seasons. When a person becomes active, the body seems to sense a need to get lighter to allow the activity to take place. In a study at Stanford, a group of inactive men began a jogging program, which increased their appetite by about 300 calories per day (a total of 2100 calories a week). Interestingly, they used only 200 calories per day, 5 days a week in their jogging program (a total of 1000 calories) so that they ended up with a positive energy balance of about 1100 calories per week. According to traditional thought they should have gained weight—but they *lost* weight instead.

Method of Weight Loss	Composition of Weight Change		
	Fat	*Other Cells*	*Fluids*
Dieting Alone	75%	10%	15%
Starvation	50%	50%	0%
Diet plus exercise	98%	− 10%	2%

FIGURE 3–5 Weight loss ratio with dieting, starvation, and diet plus exercise. (Adapted from Shephard, Roy J. *Alive Man,* Charles C. Thomas, 1972)

2. Jogging can help maintain lean body mass (LBM). Why is this important? You must realize that fat can be eliminated from the body *only* by the metabolic action of cells (primarily muscle cells) which use it for energy. Dieting can actually cause as much muscle loss as fat loss (see Figure 3–5) and less muscle means fewer places for fat to be burned. One woman who had been on a restricted intake diet for several years to maintain her size 10 figure had lost over 20 pounds of LBM in the process. Beginning a jogging program helped her gain back the LBM while eating normally. After 4 months of exercise and proper eating, she gained the LBM back and lost the excess fat *without gaining or losing any weight.*

3. Jogging stimulates muscles to burn fat. Research has shown that inactive people have a poor supply of fat-burning enzymes and that exercise can increase these enzyme levels so that fat is burned more readily. Joggers become better fat burners and this change helps them lose fat.

4. Jogging also uses a lot of energy.

   Exercise has not been accepted as a method for losing weight because it has been thought that too much work is required to lose a pound of fat. For instance, someone has said that you must chop wood for 7 hours or walk for 14 hours to lose only 1 pound of fat. If your goal is to lose one pound of fat in a very short time, it is not the way. However, exercise can have a very substantial effect over the long haul. Table 3–3 shows the effect of a daily caloric inbalance over a period of a year. For example, using only 96 calories a day would burn the number of calories contained in 10 pounds of fat each year. This is equivalent to less than 10 minutes of jogging per day.

   The cumulative effect of the recommended jogging program of this text will result in the use of an extra 300 to 500 kcals per day. This type of imbalance could theoretically yield from 25 to 50 pounds of fat loss per year or allow a thin person to eat an extra piece of pie or dish of ice cream a day with no change in weight.

It is a common misconception that diet is the sole answer to weight loss. What does recent research tell us about the role of exercise?

TABLE 3–3 CALORIC IMBALANCE TABLE

9.6 calories used each day	1 lb. lost per year
19.2 ” ”	2 ” ”
28.8 ” ”	3 ” ”
38.4 ” ”	4 ” ”
48.0 ” ”	5 ” ”
57.6 ” ”	6 ” ”
67.2 ” ”	7 ” ”
76.8 ” ”	8 ” ”
86.4 ” ”	9 ” ”
96.0 ” ”	10 ” ”
105.6 ” ”	11 ” ”
115.2 ” ”	12 ” ”
124.8 ” ”	13 ” ”
134.4 ” ”	14 ” ”
144.0 ” ”	15 ” ”
153.6 ” ”	16 ” ”
163.2 ” ”	17 ” ”
172.8 ” ”	18 ” ”
182.4 ” ”	19 ” ”
192.0 ” ”	20 ” ”
201.6 ” ”	21 ” ”
211.2 ” ”	22 ” ”
220.8 ” ”	23 ” ”
230.4 ” ”	24 ” ”
240.0 ” ”	25 ” ”

Table 3–4 shows the number of calories used each minute when running at different speeds. You can use this information to calculate the total number of calories you use each day with your program.

It is clear that exercise is the *first* step in successful weight control.

Of course, if you are overweight and have been inactive for some time, it is important to follow the "How to Begin" guidelines in Chapter 2. Don't be in a hurry to get to the jogging phase. Walk until you have begun to lose weight and have toughened your body for several weeks.

TABLE 3-4 CALORIE EXPENDITURE PER MINUTE FOR RUNNING AT DIFFERENT SPEEDS

	Body Weight in Lbs.																					
	90	99	108	117	125	134	143	152	161	170	178	187	196	205	213	222	231	240	249	257	266	275
Running, 11-min. mile 5.5 mph	6.4	7.1	7.7	8.3	9.0	9.6	10.2	10.8	11.5	12.1	12.7	13.4	14.0	14.6	15.2	15.9	16.5	17.1	17.8	18.4	19.0	19.6
Running, 8.5-min. mile 7 mph	8.4	9.2	10.0	10.8	11.7	12.5	13.3	14.1	14.9	15.7	16.6	17.4	18.2	19.0	19.8	20.7	21.5	22.3	23.1	23.9	24.8	25.6
Running, 7-min. mile 9 mph	9.3	10.2	11.1	12.9	13.1	13.9	14.8	15.7	16.6	17.5	18.9	19.3	20.2	21.1	22.1	23.0	23.9	24.8	25.7	26.6	27.5	28.4
Running, 5-min. mile 12 mph	11.8	13.0	14.1	15.3	16.4	17.6	18.7	19.9	21.0	22.2	23.3	24.5	25.6	26.8	27.9	29.1	30.2	31.4	32.5	33.7	34.9	36.0
Stationary Running, 140 counts/min.	14.6	16.1	17.5	18.9	20.4	21.8	23.2	24.6	26.1	27.5	28.9	30.4	31.8	33.2	34.6	36.1	37.5	38.9	40.4	41.8	43.2	44.6
Sprinting	13.8	15.2	16.6	17.9	19.2	20.5	21.9	23.3	24.7	26.1	27.3	28.7	30.0	31.4	32.7	34.0	35.4	36.8	38.2	39.4	40.3	42.2

Source: *Fitness for Life—An Individualized Approach*, by P. E. Allsen, J. Harrison, and B. Vance, 1976. Reprinted by permission of the publisher Wm. C. Brown, Publishers, Dubuque, Iowa 52001.

Dietary Guidelines to Lose Weight

Although the exercise factors discussed in this chapter are essential to successful weight control, certain changes in your eating habits will allow the exercise to work much more effectively.

Interestingly, it isn't the number of calories as much as the *type* of food that makes a difference. Dr. Larry Oscai and his colleagues at the University of Illinois (Chicago) fed two groups of rats exactly the same number of calories for a 60-week period. One group ate regular rat chow (a low-fat, high fiber food), and the others ate a diet similar to the typical American diet; that is, about 40% of the calories coming from fat and around 25% from sugar. Despite a similar caloric intake, carcass fat averaged 51% for the rats eating the fat-rich, high-sugar diet, and only 30% for rats eating regular rat chow. This study clearly demonstrates that severe obesity can develop even without overeating if the food is high in fats and sugars. From this type of research, it is not too surprising to note that the nutrition guidelines for weight control are to (1) decrease the total fat in the diet, (2) cut down on sugars and other sweeteners, and (3) eat more complex carbohydrates such as vegetables, fruits and grains.*

Make a guess as to the weight and percent fat of several persons. Then weigh each one and compute the estimated percent fat by the appropriate formula on page 39. Judging by the results, do you think body weight or percent fat was a better guide to these individuals' appearance?

*Interestingly, these are similar to the guidelines suggested in "Dietary Guidelines for Americans" (U.S. Dept. of Agriculture) See Chapter 4, Nutrition and Jogging.

Although the emphasis in this book is on jogging, it might be helpful to list a few simple guidelines for reducing the fats and sugars in the diet:

Reducing Fats

1. Decrease butter, margarine, spreads, and dressings.
2. Change the way you prepare foods. Use no-stick pans, avoid deep frying, cut down fats in recipes.
3. Decrease the amount of meat you eat and eat lower-fat cuts.
4. Avoid fatty dairy products such as whole-milk and cheese. Use low-fat cottage cheese and yougurt instead.
5. Look at labels for fat and avoid high-fat or creamy canned foods.

Reducing Sugars

1. Avoid sugary breakfast cereals
2. Be careful with snacks
3. Many desserts are sugary

See "How To Lower Your Fat Thermostat" (suggested readings) for more complete information concerning dietary changes for weight loss.

4 Nutrition and Jogging

Since food is the fuel for the biological machinery of the body, it seems reasonable that nutrition may play an important role in any physical activity.

The question of what to eat to improve performance is as old as the history of sports. The Greeks ate large quantities of meat to replenish the loss of "muscle substance." Primitive tribes often developed food taboos as success or failure followed certain eating habits. Modern athletes have ingested large quantities of vitamins on the theory that "if a little is needed, a lot will be better." The full circle of fads has recently been reached as weight lifters and others have eaten large quantities of powdered protein, often in conjunction with steroids or other substances.

The question is: Are there really any "miracle foods" that should be eaten by athletes in any sport? The answer is: No! A good diet, based on a large variety of foods from each of the basic food groups, will meet all of the nutritional requirements of the jogger.

WHAT IS A GOOD DIET?

In 1957, the U.S. Department of Agriculture suggested that Americans should include foods from four basic food groups in their daily diet. The four basic food groups listed were: (1) milk, (2) meat, (3) bread and cereals, and (4) fruits and vegetables. In recognition of the need for more fruits, vegetables, and whole-grain cereal in the diet, the basic four groups were expanded to eight: (1) milk, (2) meat (including fish, poultry, cheese, eggs), (3) dark green or deep yellow vegetables, (4) citrus fruits, (5) other fruits and vegetables, (6) bread (consisting of whole-grain or enriched flour), (7) cereal and potatoes, and (8) fats (butter, margarine, etc.). The goal of these later guidelines was to decrease the amount of meat, fat, and refined carbohydrates (sugars) in the diet and increase the amount of vegetables, grains, and fruits we eat. These changes can surely be recommended in terms of the guidelines of the American Heart Association that have suggested lower fat levels for years, and more recently the guidelines from the American Cancer Society, who suggest decreasing the total fat intake, eating more fiber containing foods, especially vegetables containing vitamins A and C, and cruciferous vegetables (such as cauliflower, brussels sprouts, and cabbage).

In *Dietary Guidelines for Americans* (U.S. Dept. of Agriculture and U.S. Dept. of Health and Human Services, 2nd Ed. 1985), similar guidelines were given:

1. Eat a variety of foods. You need more than 40 different nutrients for good health, including vitamins and minerals, amino acids (from protein), essential fatty acids (from fats and oils), and sources of energy (calories from carbohydrates, fats, and proteins). Adequate amounts of these nutrients can be found only in a diet selected from each of the major food groups. The guidelines point out that fruits and vegetables are good sources of vitamin A, vitamin C, folic acid, fiber, and many minerals. Whole-grain and enriched breads, cereals and other grain products provide B vitamins, iron, protein, calories, and fiber. Meats, poultry, fish, and eggs supply protein, fat, iron, and other minerals, as well as several B vitamins. Dairy products are major sources of calcium and many other nutrients.

2. Maintain Desirable Weight. If you are too fat, your chances of developing some chronic disorders are increased. Obesity is associated with high blood pressure, increased levels of blood fats (triglycerides) and cholesterol, heart disease, strokes, the most common types of diabetes, certain cancers, and many other types of ill health. Thus, "you should try to maintain a 'desirable' weight" (see chapter on jogging and weight control).

3. Avoid too much fat, saturated fat, and cholesterol. Populations like ours with diets relatively high in fat (especially saturated fat) and cholesterol tend to have high blood cholesterol levels which leads to greatly increased risks of heart disease and certain cancers. Although there is some controversy regarding who should lower the levels of fat in the diet, this publication suggested that it would be "sensible" to reduce daily consumption of fat, especially in individuals who have heart disease risk factors or family histories of heart disease.

4. Eat foods with adequate starch and fiber. It is clear that the American diet is too low in dietary fiber (the part of plant foods which is generally not digestible by humans). Eating high-fiber foods has been found to reduce symptoms of chronic constipation, diverticular disease, and some types of "irritable bowel" problems. It may also reduce the chance of developing cancer of the colon. Suggested advice, is to increase your fiber intake by eating more whole-grain breads and cereals, fruits, and vegetables.

5. Avoid too much sugar. Sugar not only is related to increased problems with tooth decay, but also contains almost no nutrients and is sometimes called "empty" calories. Thus, diets with large amounts of sugars should be avoided, especially by people with low calorie needs, such as those on weight-reducing diets and the elderly.

6. Avoid too much sodium. There is a major hazard with excess sodium for people who have high blood pressure, and in populations with a low sodium intake, high blood pressure is uncommon. Since most Americans eat more sodium than is needed, consider reducing the sodium intake in your diet.

7. If you drink alcoholic beverages, do so in moderation. These beverages are high in calories and low in nutrients and are associated with serious diseases such as cirrhosis of the liver and certain types of cancer, especially in those who also smoke. Excessive use of alcohol by pregnant women may cause birth defects or other problems during pregnancy.

It has been estimated that the body needs "more than" 50 different nutrients. The only way a person can get all of them is by eating a wide variety from all of the basic groups.

Dr. Thomas Bassler, representing the American Medical Jogger's point of view, has stated that no special foods or diet supplements are needed by the jogger. He recommended, however, that highly refined foods be avoided (sugar, starch, alcohol) and that preference be given to a well-balanced diet which includes fresh fruit and raw vegetables, and a smaller portion of meat than is usually eaten. This advice is certainly in harmony with the "Dietary Guidelines for Americans" just discussed.

Nutritionists are critical of the typical American diet. For which foods do they recommend an increase in consumption and for which ones a decrease?

FOOD FOR ENERGY

It is important to realize that the body gains energy from all the food that it ingests. However, because of the way the metabolic systems work, some foods are more important to certain activities than others. For instance, at rest the body gets about equal energy from fats and carbohydrates. Once exercise starts, carbohydrates contribute more of the energy as the intensity of the exercise increases. In long term exercise, fats again begin to play a more major role.

In this section we will discuss the role of carbohydrates, fats, and proteins as they relate to the energy needs of the body during exercise.

Carbohydrates

Recent research has clearly shown the importance of carbohydrates to performances of long duration (greater than an hour). At a fairly high work load (75 percent of maximum) a runner could run for 115 minutes on a normal mixed diet (carbohydrates, fat, and protein). On a high fat, high protein diet (almost no carbohydrates), the time dropped to 60 minutes. When the diet was changed to almost pure carbohydrate, the time at the original workload increased to 170 minutes (5).

Other studies have shown that although running speed is not increased, the length of time the speed can be maintained is increased in direct proportion to the amount of carbohydrate stored in the muscles. This stored carbohydrate is called *muscle glycogen* and is a very important source of fuel for long distance running. The reason it is so important is that it is more efficient to use than is fat.

Biopsy studies, where a needle is pushed into the muscle to obtain a small sample of tissue, have shown that the muscle glycogen levels can be increased several different ways: (This procedure is called carbohydrate loading.) (1) You can "load" by simply increasing the ratio of carbohydrates you ingest. (2) You can deplete muscle glycogen by severe work, and then eat a high carbohydrate diet. (3) You can first deplete muscle glycogen, eat a low carbohydrate diet for several days, and then go on a high carbohydrate diet. Using method (1) or (2) would surely be effective for all but the most highly trained, world class athlete. In fact, for runs of less than an hour's duration, carbohydrate loading would make very little difference in performance.

Some runners have tried to store extra carbohydrates by eating sugar or honey just before a race. This is an unwise practice and may cause cramps and nausea. The excess sugar often stimulates the production of insulin, and may leave you with a lower blood sugar level than before.

Drinking certain of the "aid" drinks during a race can actually have a negative effect. First, if the concentration of sugar is greater than about 2.5 percent, the movement of the fluid into the system will be slowed and you may experience problems with dehydration even though you have fluid in the stomach. Second, since sweating causes a larger loss of fluid than electrolytes (sodium, potassium, etc.), the "aid" drinks might actually cause a super-saturation of these minerals. For most situations, water is the best replacement fluid while jogging. Most of the minerals can easily be replaced in the normal diet after the race is over, and are not needed during the race itself.

Why is drinking water during a race preferable to drinking one of the "aid" drinks?

Fats

Because of the emphasis on carbohydrates, the value of fat as a source of energy has often been underestimated. It is important to realize that fat is an important source of energy while jogging, and becomes more important as the duration increases.

The amount of fat used depends primarily on the intensity of the work and on your physical conditioning level. Fat requires oxygen to release its energy, whereas carbohydrates can yield energy anaerobically (without oxygen). If we run at high intensities, the body is forced to use carbohydrates because insufficient oxygen is available to burn fats only. Training increases our ability to use fat for energy as the mitochondria (energy factories in the cell) increase not only their size and capacity but also the amount of fat burning enzymes they contain.

One thing to remember, too much fat is known to be detrimental to health and both the American Heart Association and the American Cancer Society have recommended that Americans decrease the amount of fat in the diet. This in no way decreases your ability to use fats for energy during jogging. At any given time, most of us have from 75,000 to 125,000 calories worth of energy stored in the fat cells of the body, and we do not need to seek fats to increase our endurance. In fact, the essential fats are all "unsaturated" fats and are found in grains and vegetables rather than animal and dairy products. If you avoid all the fats you can, you will still get from 20 to 25 percent of your calories from this source because of the hidden nature of so many fats.

Proteins

Early attempts to evaluate the role of proteins as a source of fuel used a measure of nitrogen excretion to determine that only about 5 to 10 percent of the energy came from this source. However, later research has shown that the role of amino acids (small protein molecules) may be more important to the overall energy picture than originally thought. Apparently, even though these small protein molecules contribute little to the overall energy needs, they are important to the function of the energy pathways themselves.

The question of whether extra protein is needed by an active person in training is still not completely answered. Most scientists feel that a dietary protein intake of between .8 and 1.0 grams per kilogram of body weight is plenty (your body weight in kilograms is equal to your weight in pounds times .453). Most athletes and joggers eat this much and more. However, some recent studies have shown that athletes often go into negative nitrogen balance during the initiation stages of exercise and it may be a good idea to increase the protein intake during the first week or two of training to 1.5 to 2.0 grams per kilogram per day. After that time, the nitrogen balance returns to normal and the natural increase in protein associated with increased total food intake will more than satisfy the need.

PRECOMPETITION MEAL

Much has been written regarding the "pre-game" meal and many false ideas have been taught by well-meaning coaches and athletes. For joggers, a moderate, well-balanced meal should be eaten about 2½ to 3 hours prior to running, especially if you are competing in a fun-run. This meal should emphasize carbohydrates, but not pure sugars. The idea that hotcakes and syrup with chocolate bars and candy are good for any precompetition meal is false. The meal you eat should consist of things you enjoy eating and that your body is used to receiving. A small piece of meat, a baked potato (without too much butter), vegetable, roll, milk or juice remains an excellent choice for the average person. The complex carbohydrates in the potato and whole grain roll are much better than syrups and pancakes because they are digested more slowly and their energy is released like a time capsule.

In summary, joggers should eat a normal well-balanced diet, that is low in fat and sugar and high in complex carbohydrates such as vegetables, fruits, and grains. If you jog less than an hour a day, no special loading techniques are necessary. You should allow 2 to 2½ hours after eating so that the food is digested.

In longer events (one to two hours), it may be wise to increase the ratio of carbohydrates for several days prior to the event to increase the muscle glycogen levels.

For events longer than two hours (such as a marathon), it may be a good idea to consume moderate amounts of sugar during the race itself to help maintain blood sugar levels. This could be consumed along with the liquid used for rehydration, but should be no more than 1½ tablespoons of sugar per 1 quart of water (about 2 percent in commercial drinks).

5 Principles of Aerobic Conditioning

This chapter has been read.

Two of the key words of the education process are "how" and "why." Most of this book has involved the "how" of jogging. It is not necessary to read this chapter to know how to jog successfully. However, if you are interested in some of the scientific aspects of jogging, read on.

PHYSIOLOGY OF JOGGING

Every cell in the body is a small combustion engine, and like an engine, needs oxygen to burn as fuel for the production of energy. The more oxygen available to the cells, the more energy can be produced. The more energy produced, the greater the ability to do work. Work that can be done for long periods of time is called aerobic (literally, with oxygen) work.

Since oxygen is carried by the hemoglobin in the blood, your capacity to do aerobic work is related to the amount of blood you can pump through the cardiovascular system. Since the heart is the organ which pumps the blood, exercises which benefit the heart will develop aerobic capacity.

The heart is a muscle and responds to training like any other muscle of the body. To train any muscle, you must "overload" it or push it beyond its normal load. For example, to train the biceps, a person would do bicep curls with a heavy weight. The problem is finding a way to overload the heart.

To understand how this principle applies to training the heart, you must understand something about how the heart functions.

As the heart beats at rest, only part of the blood inside the ventricle is ejected. The amount of blood ejected each time the heart beats is called "stroke volume." As we begin to jog, the heart beats faster and with greater force, and more blood is ejected with each beat. This increased stroke volume, along with the increased in heart rate, allows the body to increase the total blood flow from around five liters per minute at rest, to twenty or thirty liters per minute during very intense work. As the amount of blood ejected from the heart is increased, the load on the heart muscle becomes greater. This increase in load is thought to be the stimulus which causes the heart muscle to become stronger and more efficient.

Fortunately, maximum exercise is not required to overload the heart. Your maximum stroke volume, or best overload, probably occurs about halfway between resting and maximum work. This means that normal jogging elicits an effective overload on your heart muscle even though you are not maximally stressed. This fact explains the excellent training effect associated with jogging even though the work load is moderate and feels comfortable.

Another requirement for training the heart effectively is to use an activity which involves the large muscles of the body and which is rhythmic and continuous. This type of activity is effective because it encourages the return of blood to the heart, for there is no overload without blood. When jogging, the veins of the large leg muscles fill as the leg is relaxed and them empty toward the heart as the leg is again rhythmically contracted. The action of the valves in the veins insures that the blood will be pushed toward the heart and will not return to the feet as it would if the valves were not present.

Changes occur in the muscles as well as in the heart. Increases in the amount of oxygen pumped by the heart would be of little value if there were no systems in the muscles to use the extra oxygen to produce energy. In the muscle cells, energy is produced by the mitochondria. These small "power-plants" have specific enzymes which break apart the food particles, changing the energy in the food to adenosine triphosphate (ATP), a high energy compound used by the body for muscular contraction. Research has shown that jogging is an effective way to develop more and better mitochondria. With the increase in the number of mitochondria and an increased supply of oxygen, the energy available for work is increased dramatically.

The amount of energy you can produce at maximal work is called your "aerobic capacity" or Vo_2 max. The measurement of aerobic capacity requires special equipment which measures the volume of air you breathe and analyzes it for oxygen and carbon dioxide content while you run or walk on a motor driven treadmill. High levels indicate excellent cardiovascular fitness. Great endurance runners can use as much as 85 milliliters of oxygen for each kilogram of body

weight each minute (85 ml/kg/min). The average college student will use be-tween 40 and 50 ml/kg/min and many adults may have only 20 to 30 ml/kg/min capacities. Obviously, low capacities are a real limitation to your ability to enjoy life. People with low capacities huff and puff with even minor exertion, and sometimes shy away from fun activities because they are unable to provide enough energy to support these activities. You can estimate your oxygen uptake capacity by using the Sharkey Step Test or the Cooper's Test found in chapter 1. Regular jogging will increase this capacity after only a month or so.

Acute Response to Jogging

It might be interesting for you to know more about your body and about some of the changes that occur as you begin to jog.

Heart Rate   As a person begins to jog, the heart rate goes up to increase the supply of oxygen (which is carried by the hemoglobin) to the muscle cells. During low-level jogging, the heart rate will usually attain a plateau or steady-state within a few minutes. If you increase the speed, the heart rate will go up. The relation-ship between heart rate and work load is fairly linear.

At any steady-state workload, the heart rate of a trained person will be lower than that of an untrained person. This is because the trained heart is stronger and pumps more blood with each beat. Therefore, fewer beats per minute are necessary to supply the same amount of oxygen at any given speed (see Figure 5-1).

At progressively higher running rates, one will eventually attain a level which will exhaust even the most fit individual. Prior to this point, the heart rate will reach and level off at its maximum rate. This rate can be predicted by subtracting your age from 220. Your maximum heart rate may be slightly different from a friend of the same age, because there are some individual differences between people of the same age. However, these differences are not large ($\pm$ 10 beats), and the maximum heart rate as predicted from this formula can be used effec-tively to compute your training heart rate (see Chapter 2). Maximum heart rate decreases about 1 beat per year after age 20.

The *resting heart rate varies* according to fitness level, environmental fac-tors, body position, age, etc. However, most well-trained athletes have extremely low resting heart rates of from 35 to 40 beats per minute. Jogging will lower your resting heart rate too.

Stroke Volume   As mentioned before, stroke volume is the amount of blood pumped by the heart with each beat. There are several factors which influence the amount of blood that the heart can eject: one is the size of the ventricle itself. Jogging will increase the size of your ventricle. Another factor is the amount of force the heart can exert as it pumps. This is related to the strength of the heart muscle, and this strength is increased by jogging. The third and perhaps the most important factor is the amount of blood returning to the heart. Exercises which are rhythmic and squeeze the veins of the muscles in the lower legs tend to return large quantities of blood and help increase stroke volume.

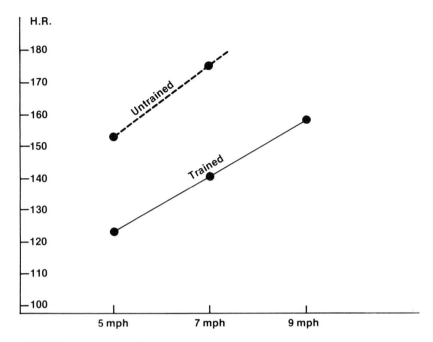

FIGURE 5–1 Exercise heart rate response of trained and untrained subjects at 3 different speeds.

Cardiac Output   Cardiac output is the total amount of blood the heart is able to pump each minute. It increases linearly with increases in work level to the point of exhaustion. The real difference between well-trained runners and those who are poorly conditioned is the amount of cardiac output or blood that can be pumped each minute to the muscles of the body. The resting cardiac output for most people is from 4 to 6 liters per minute, and the maximum values are about 20 to 30 liters per minute in normal people and may be as high as 40 liters per minute in extremely well-trained individuals.

Blood Flow   The blood pumped by the heart is directed to various parts of the body depending on tissue need. During exercise, blood is shunted to those areas of highest metabolic need (the muscles) and is closed off to those areas where there is little or no metabolic activity (such as the gut). On hot days the skin receives some of the blood to help cool the body. The blood flow to the skin decreases the amount of blood available to the muscles and explains why you must jog more slowly on hot days.

Blood Pressure   Blood pressure is the pressure of the blood in the vessels when the heart beats (systolic) and between beats (diastolic). At rest, the normal pressure is about 120 mmHg systolic and 80 mmHg diastolic (120/80). During work the systolic pressure rises dramatically and may be as high as 200 to 250 mmHg. Very little change occurs in the diastolic pressure in normal subjects during work.

Respiratory Response   The purpose of the lungs is to provide a source of oxygen for the blood and to allow the blood to release the carbon dioxide picked up from the working cells. The normal volume of air moved out of the lungs each minute at rest is about 5 liters. During exercise, this volume can be increased to 100 liters for normal people and up to 200 liters per minute for large, well-trained athletes. Normal breathing frequency is 10 to 15 times per minute at rest and 45 to 60 times per minute at maximal work. The amount of air moved from the lungs each breath (tidal volume) varies, depending upon the size of the individual. However, normal tidal volume is about a half-liter at rest and increases to about one half of your vital capacity (VC) during maximal work. The lungs have more than enough capacity to handle any amount of work we can do. The feeling of being "short of breath" when you exercise is a problem of blood supply and not of respiration.

All of the air that comes into the lungs must be cleaned, warmed, and saturated. The cleaning is done by small hair-like projections called cilia. When particles are trapped on the inner bronchi, these small cilia beat rhythmically and push the particles out of the lungs. The air is warmed to 37° C as it comes into contact with the inner part of the body, and water is added to saturate the air by special mucous cells called "goblet cells." These cells are sometimes overloaded at high workload in cold temperatures as they try to produce enough mucous to saturate the air. Under these conditions, we may have a dry, raspy cough and some pain in the lungs after running.

As you jog, approximately how much increase over the resting state occurs in heart rate and in stroke volume?

After jogging in cold temperatures at a fast pace, the runner may experience a dry cough and pain in the lungs. What is the cause of this discomfort?

Chronic Adaptations to Jogging

The body makes some very interesting adaptations to the stress of jogging. These occur specifically to provide more energy to the body during work. A summary of the important changes are listed in Table 5–1. You don't need to understand these changes to benefit from your jogging program, but you may be interested in them from an intellectual point of view.

In comparing trained and untrained individuals, what differences would you expect to find in relation to heart rate at rest and at steady-state workloads, aerobic capacity, maximum heart rate, diastolic blood pressure, and stroke volume? Which differences are minor?

TABLE 5-1   EFFECTS OF ENDURANCE TRAINING

Hypothetical Physiological and Body Composition Changes in a Sedentary Normal Individual Resulting from an Endurance Training Program,[1] Compared to the Values of a World-Class Endurance Runner of the Same Age

Variables	Sedentary Normal		World-Class Endurance Runner
	Pre- Training	*Post- Training*	
Cardiovascular			
HRrest, beats/min	71	59	36
HRmax, beats/min	185	183	174
SVrest, ml[2]	65	80	125
SVmax, ml[2]	120	140	200
Qrest, liters/min	4.6	4.7	4.5
Qmax, liters/min	22.2	25.6	34.8
Heart volume, ml	750	820	1,200
Blood volume, liters	4.7	5.1	6.0
Systolic BPrest, mmHg	135	130	12.0
Systolic BPmax, mmHg	210	205	210
Diastolic BPrest, mmHg	78	76	65
Diastolic BPmax, mmHg	82	80	65
Respiratory			
VErest, liters/min (BTPS)	7	6	6
VEmax, liters/min (BTPS)	110	135	195
f rest, breaths/min	14	12	12
f max, breaths/min	40	45	55
TVrest, liters	0.5	0.5	0.5
TVmax, liters	2.75	3.0	0.5
VC, liters	5.8	6.0	6.2
RV, liters	1.4	1.2	1.2
Metabolic			
a-vO$_2$ diff rest, ml/100 ml	6.0	6.0	6.0
a-vO$_2$ diff max, ml/100 ml	14.5	15.0	16.0
Vo$_2$ rest, ml/kg/min	3.5	3.7	4.0
Vo$_2$ max, ml/kg/min	40.5	49.8	76.7
Blood lactate rest, mg/100 ml	10	10	10
Blood lactate max, mg/100 ml	110	125	185
Body Composition			
Weight, lb	175	170	150
Fat Weight, lb	28	21.3	11.3
Lean Weight, 1 lb	147	148.7	138.7
Relative Fat, %	16.0	12.5	7.5

[1]6-month training program, jogging 3–4 times/week, 30 min/day, at 75% of his Vo$_2$ max.
[2]Upright position.
Source: The Heart and Lungs at Work by Jack H. Wilmore and Allen L. Norton, copyright 1974. Reprinted by permisson of Beckman Instruments, Inc. Schiller Park, Ill 60176

Cardiovascular   First, note that total heart volume increases with training. This increase results from an increase in interior dimensions as well as hypertrophy of the heart muscle itself.

Since the heart can hold more blood, the amount pushed out each beat (stroke volume) at rest is larger. This larger stroke volume at rest allows the heart to pump the same volume each minute with fewer beats. The decrease in resting heart rate shown in Table 5–1 is quite typical following a few months of training. Note the resting heart rate of the endurance athlete. As the stroke volume gets larger, the heart rate decreases.

The larger heart volume is also helpful at any submaximal work level. Since the stroke volume is larger, the heart rate at any work level is lower in the trained as compared with the untrained. This means that the relative intensity for the trained is less at any work load.

The maximum heart rate changes very little with training. In fact, it might decrease slightly. Yet the total output of the heart is much greater. This is because of the larger volume of the ventricle and the increased contractile force of the muscle associated with training. The heart muscle is like other muscles in that it grows stronger with training and is able to pump blood more efficiently. This allows it to empty almost completely the ventricle each time it beats during maximum work. An untrained heart cannot do this.

Little blood pressure change occurs in normal subjects, but hypertense individuals often experience a decrease in their high blood pressure as they train. Maximal blood pressure is quite similar in the trained and untrained.

Total blood volume usually increases slightly as a result of jogging. This increases the total amount of hemoglobin available to carry oxygen.

Respiratory   Resting breathing patterns change very little following a training program, although at submaximal work there is usually a small increase in pulmonary ventilation (VE). The big change in VE occurs during maximum work. Trained individuals have much greater capacity to move air into and out of the lungs. Total vital capacity (VC) also increases. There is little change in tidal volume (TV) or residual volume (RV).

Metabolic   There are significant increases in maximal oxygen consumption (VO_2) in trained individuals. The amount of increase can be as much as 25 percent. The increase is associated with the increase in the amount of blood pumped past the cells, and to the changes which occur in the cells to use the extra oxygen. Of course, an increase in VO_2 max allows a person to produce much more energy than before. This extra energy can be used to jog farther and faster, and it makes other physical tasks much easier to perform. There is little change in the amount of oxygen extracted from the circulating blood (a-vO_2 diff).

Body Composition   One of the most rewarding features associated with jogging is the decrease in total body fat. The 3.5 percent decrease in Table 5–1 is fairly typical and represents about 7 pounds of fat in this example. Note that total weight did not change drastically, so we know that the muscle mass was conserved while the fat was lost. Usually, joggers lose inches around the waist and hips as the fat goes off.

Biochemical   Many changes occur in the muscles to help the body perform better. These changes increase the capacity of skeletal muscles to oxidize glucose and fat for energy during work. Not only is there an increase in the number and size of the mitochondria, but the enzymes in the metabolic pathways increase in activity and number.

Jogging also increases the amount of glycogen in the muscle. This provides a steady source of energy to the muscle while you jog. Trained muscle can also use fats more easily. This change makes the system more able to work for longer periods of time without fatigue.

6 Motivation, Incentives and Racing Competition

MOTIVATION

By now it is assumed that you are becoming committed to the activity of jogging, but there may come a time when it might be difficult to motivate yourself to exercise. It has been the experience of the authors that there are some basic tips that help people to continue with their exercise program. These suggestions may be helpful in making jogging a continuing life style.

Work Out with a Friend   One of the pleasures of exercise is its social interaction. Also, having another person depend on you makes it harder to procrastinate.

Don't Over-exercise   One of the common mistakes of a beginning jogger is the tendency to overwork. It takes time for the body to respond to the training effect. George Sheehan, M.D., a noted cardiologist and long distance runner, states that you should listen to your body. If you are tired, listless, and suffering from fatigue on the day following your jog, you should back off and not drive yourself so hard. Remember, exercise should be enjoyable and add to the pleasure of life.

Work Out in Different Places   You can increase the enjoyment you receive from jogging by choosing several different areas for your run. Too often, people jog around and around the same quarter-mile running track. You live in a beautiful world. By changing your running environment, you can add spice to your exercise.

Start Workouts at the Same Time Each Day   People are creatures of habit and by selecting a specific time to jog, you will be more prone to continue your program. Schedule your exercise as an important part of your daily life, and in time it will become an important part of your day, one that you will look forward to.

Set a Goal   By having a specific goal to work toward, you can periodically determine if you are making progress. Some people determine how many miles they wish to jog by a certain date or a specific time so many days a week.

A jogger is well advised to listen to the body. What does this advice mean?

Keep a Progress Chart   Keeping a simple progress chart will help you evaluate the consistency of your jogging program. For some reason, people do better when they set goals and then record their progress. You do not need to keep elaborate records; a simple sheet can be used to compile a great amount of information that will be interesting to you in the future. Record such things as the distance run, the best day during your best week or month and how you felt. Table 6–1 is an example of a chart that could be used.

Concentrate on Success   The word "success" is derived from the Latin verb "succedere" which means to do well. Thus, a person who does well can be said to be successful. You do not need to defeat another person to be successful, as success is always relative. Perhaps our greatest success is when we achieve victory over ourselves. This success becomes purely personal and is not something that can be measured only by the distance run and the time recorded.

ORGANIZATIONS AND INCENTIVE PROGRAMS

President's Council   In order to motivate the average citizen to a life of activity, the President's Council on Physical Fitness and Sports has sponsored the Presidential Sports Award Program. The Presidential Award is offered for most popular sports including jogging. The program is open to both males and females, and you do not have to be highly skilled to qualify. Participation is the important thing. When you qualify for the Presidential Sports Award, you will receive a handsome enameled pin, a colorful embroidered emblem, and a certificate bearing the President's signature and seal. Information on the program, including qualifying standards, application forms, and personal logbooks, may be obtained free by writing to Presidential Sports Award, P.O. Box 129, Radio City Station, New York, NY, 10019.

American Running and Fitness Association   The American Running and Fitness Association is an organization that grew out of the National Jogging Association that was founded in 1968. This organization has provided a great service by providing information and motivation concerning physical fitness. It has been especially helpful in promoting jogging as a most practical and economical way for a large number of people to achieve and maintain physical fitness.

The association publishes a monthly newsletter that contains a wealth of information ranging from topics about aerobic exercise, jogging benefits, diet, and other fitness knowledge. This provides the reader with timely and reliable information to keep them up-to-date on the latest research about sportsmedicine, fitness, and exercise.

They also provide an answer service where members can send questions and receive individual answers concerning any aspect of health and fitness.

Information concerning the organization can be obtained by writing the American Running and Fitness Association, 2001 S Street, N.W., Suite 540, Washington, D.C. 20009.

TABLE 6–1 INDIVIDUAL PROGRESS CHARTS

Best Weeks	Total Jogging Time	Distance	Comments
1.			
2.			
3.			
4.			
5.			
6.			
7.			
8.			
9.			
10			

Best Days	Total Jogging Time	Distance	Comments
1.			
2			
3.			
4.			
5.			
6.			
7.			
8.			
9.			
10.			

Best Months	Total Jogging Time	Distance	Comments
1.			
2.			
3.			
4.			
5.			
6.			
7.			
8.			
9.			
10.			

FUN RUNS

Runner's World magazine has promoted an idea that does much to encourage beginning runners. They call these events "fun runs" and the idea is to strip the organizational work to the bare essentials and provide a fun activity for the maximum number of people.

They recommend that the following format be followed in order to have successful runs.

1. Runs every week on a Saturday or Sunday morning, starting early enough so the day is still cool and the traffic not heavy.
2. No registration before the runs.
3. No entry fees if possible. If a fee is charged, just make it an amount to cover the cost of certificates.
4. No restrictions on entries.
5. Distances from a half-mile to five miles on accurately measured, easy-to-follow, and not too difficult courses.
6. Times for each runner read from a running watch with nothing recorded. A times reader can be recruited by a member of someone's family who isn't running.
7. Printed certificates to all finishers that are color-coded for time standards. For example, a five minute or below mile is gold, six minutes is blue, seven minutes is red, eight and one-half minutes is green, and anything higher is white. Adjustments can be made for age and sex.

Further information concerning the organization of Fun Runs can be obtained by writing to: *Runner's World*, P.O. Box 366, Mountain View, California, 94042.

For future reference, check your local newspapers, bulletin boards, posters, etc. for news of running competitions. Start a list of upcoming events and of organizations that sponsor runs.

STEPPING UP TO RACING COMPETITION

After a person has been jogging for some time he or she realizes the benefits that come with such a program; these include increased fitness of heart and circulatory-respiratory systems, and the loss of excess fat. Then the jogger may want to test the new found fitness in a more competitive environment. Racing is available to almost any person of any age or sex and of varying abilities. The races that are available run the spectrum from the localized fun type runs to races involving world-class competitors.

Training

Before you begin competitive racing, you may need to increase your training distance. The question of how much training is necessary for any given distance is not an easy one to answer. Ken Young, one of the outstanding long distance runners in the United States, has put together a "Collapse Point" table which is thought to predict when a runner will reach his racing limit as determined by previous training. Although the term "Collapse Point" sounds ominous, it merely refers to the point where further running would be difficult. Your limit is approximately "three times your average daily distance for the past 6–8 weeks." If you have averaged 28 miles during the past 6–8 weeks, then your daily average would be 4 miles and your maximum effective distance would be 12 miles. Mr. Young recommends training at a distance greater than the minimum projected racing distance in order to give yourself a safety margin. See Table 6–2 for the collapse point guidelines he recommends.

TABLE 6–2 "COLLAPSE POINTS"

Basic Mileage Requirements

Weekly Total	Per Day	"Collapse"	Max. Race
10 miles	1½ miles	5 miles	3 miles
15 miles	2¼ miles	7 miles	5 miles
20 miles	3 miles	9 miles	6 miles
25 miles	3½ miles	11 miles	8 miles
30 miles	4¼ miles	13 miles	10 miles
35 miles	5 miles	15 miles	13 miles*
40 miles	5¾ miles	17 miles	15 miles
45 miles	6½ miles	20 miles	19 miles*
50 miles	7 miles	21 miles	19 miles*
55 miles	7¾ miles	23 miles	20 miles
60 miles	8½ miles	26 miles	20 miles
65 miles	9¼ miles	28 miles	marathon
70 miles	10 miles	30 miles	marathon
75 miles	10¾ miles	32 miles	31 miles*
80 miles	11½ miles	34½ miles	31 miles*
85 miles	12¼ miles	37 miles	31 miles*
90 miles	12¾ miles	39 miles	31 miles*
95 miles	13½ miles	41 miles	31 miles*
100 miles	14¼ miles	43 miles	31 miles*

"Collapse point" is approximately three times the daily average; maximum racing distance should be slightly below the collapse point. * = 20 kilometers is slightly less than 13 miles, the half-marathon slightly more; 30 kilometers is just below 19 miles; 31 miles is about 50 kilometers.
Reprinted with permission from *Step Up to Racing* published by *Runner's World* Magazine/World Publications, Mountain View, Ca. p. 13.

Dr. Jack Scaff, a cardiologist from Hawaii who has been successful in training adults to run the Honolulu marathon, uses training distances similar to those found in the Collapse Point table. His philosophy of training was summarized in *Sports Illustrated* (10).

He stresses that the marathon is "only an excuse to get people running and to give them a goal." His guidelines for preparation revolve around training "finishers," not racers.

He maintains that most people run too fast during training. "If you can't run for an hour," says Scaff, "you're running too fast." The minute you can't talk, you're running too fast. "The minute you can't talk, you're sprinting." He thinks a good initial pace for most beginners may be nine to ten minutes per mile or slower. He encourages his runners to begin running an hour three times a week as soon as possible (30 miles per week). After 5 months of this type of training, he begins to increase the distance to 40 miles per week (4 training sessions) for about a month; then to 50 miles per week; and finally to 60 miles a week for the last 60 days before the marathon.

His rule of thumb is that the total mileage for the last 60 days divided by 20 will tell you how many miles you can run at your training pace. For instance, if you have run 60 miles a week for the last 60 days, or 480 miles, you can run 24 miles at your training pace (480 ÷ 20). If you have run 520 miles the last 60 days, you can finish the 26 miles at your regular training pace (520 ÷ 20 = 26). Dr. Scaff maintains that anyone who runs 30 miles per week for 60 days prior to the marathon can finish if he or she runs 20% slower than the training pace. That means that if you normally train at 8 minutes per mile, you need to slow down to 9½ minutes per mile to finish.

Assume that you are preparing for a marathon race. You have run 30 miles per week for the last 60 days at a speed of 8.5 miles per hour. At what rate should you run in the marathon in order to finish the distance?

Running the Hills

There comes a time in every jogger's career when he or she wishes to leave the flat level terrain and look for a new experience by heading for the hills. Hill running can bring a new challenge and a different demand on the human body. By working on a few techniques you can make this an enjoyable experience, one that can open up new dimensions of fitness.

Uphill running requires a greater amount of energy, but it is an excellent method to stimulate the various systems of the body. This type of activity can strengthen the quadricep muscles, so important in running, increase the cardiovascular capacity, and help the body to adapt so that the following hill workouts will become easier. Hill running is sometimes termed "speedwork in disguise" by some runners, even though you may use a relatively slow pace going uphill and not notice a great amount of effort in the downhill phase. Dr. David Costill of Ball State University estimates that uphill running at a 6% incline requires 35% more energy expenditure than running the same distance on a flat terrain.

Running downhill helps to stretch out your stride, and the free flowing experience of running slightly out of control is a feeling of freedom that is hard to find in any other activity.

There are two basic keys to remember about running the hills. The first has to do with going uphill. The secret is to be relaxed and to lean into the hill, and to also use the arms by swinging them parallel to your direction of movement, rather than across the body. One might think of running uphill as time to "shift the gear," as it is usually necessary to shorten the stride in order to find that efficient length that will allow you to move with the least amount of effort. The best way to develop this efficient style is to practice a certain amount of hill running.

In running downhill, the key again is to be relaxed and to hold an efficient rhythm of running. Many people start to lean backwards, which causes the runner to slow down, and this is a detriment. One point to remember is to have a footplant that is flat. You should attempt to obtain a free-wheeling type of stride where you still have control, but are able to use the down-slope of the hill to enable you to pick up speed.

If you will make hill running a part of your weekly workouts, there is no need to fear the hills; they can become a very interesting and challenging part of your training routine.

Racing Information

In order to find out where various races are being held, the following list will be helpful:

1. Amateur Athletic Union—By writing to AAU House, 3400 W. 86th Street, Indianapolis, IN, 46268, you can obtain the name of the AAU Long Distance Chairman in your area. By contacting the chairman, you can obtain a list of the dates of races being sponsored by the AAU.
2. Road Runner's Club of America. The various RRCA chapters sponsor distance runs on a regular basis and information can be obtained concerning regional and national races by writing to Road Runner's Club of America, 2737 Devonshire Place NW, Washington, D.C., 20008.
3. *Runner's World* Magazine. This is a publication that has contributed a great deal to the long distance running and jogging movements. Each issue contains a list of up-coming runs in various parts of the country. Information concerning this magazine can be obtained by writing to *Runner's World,* Box 366, Mountain View, CA, 94042.
4. Local Clubs. In most areas there are local running clubs that help to organize various races. By checking the local newspapers, you should be able to locate when and where the races are held.

Some areas have no formal running clubs. In this case, you and your running friends may wish to organize a club of your own or at least organize some local road races to help promote running in your community. Appendix 2 contains all of the information you will need in order to organize an effective road race in your area.

7 Commonly Asked Questions and Answers

Through the years, the authors have kept a record of the most commonly asked questions that joggers have asked. This chapter is a compilation of these questions and answers.

Q. What is the effect of running 4–12 miles each day on the ankles, knees, and legs? Will this much jogging cause permanent damage to my body?

A. The best guide is how your body feels after a workout. If you are without pain there will be no problems. The chief causes of pain are poor shoes, improper running style, especially footplant, poor flexibility, and poor alignment of the lower body structure. There is no research data to suggest that permanent damage occurs to the body with proper and sensible jogging.

Q. When I run more than 2 miles I sometimes get chafing between the legs.

A. Use a liberal coating of petroleum jelly before you start your runs. Also the mode of support might cause a problem. Instead of the normal athletic supporter, you might consider using a snug undershort or nylon panty. One runner solved this problem by cutting the inner seam out of the running shorts, approximately two inches up from the hem and thus reduced the rubbing of the hem of the shorts on the inside of the thighs.

Q. I really want to increase my fitness and have wondered about using ankle weights to increase the resistance.

A. In many cases the weights may interfere with your natural stride and contribute to injury. You can easily increase the fitness effect by running either farther or slightly faster.

Q. I have a problem with blisters, especially on the big toe and ball of the foot.

A. First, check your shoes for a proper fit. One way to reduce friction is to apply a layer of moleskin over the area where the friction occurs.

Q. I sometimes get a stitch in the side while running; what would you suggest?

A. A "stitch" or pain in the side is probably caused by lack of oxygen to the diaphragm or some other abdominal muscle. It sometimes helps to relax consciously the abdominal area as you run. Sometimes, eating just prior to your jog will cause a pain to occur. You probably should eat 2 to 3 hours before exercising. If the pain persists, slow down to a walk for a few minutes.

Q. What are orthotics and are they helpful?
A. Orthotics are supports placed in the shoe to enable the foot to be in proper position while walking and running. It is possible to buy over-the-counter supports that may be helpful, but for continuing lower-leg pain, you should consult a sports podiatrist or an orthopedic surgeon who is knowledgeable about sports and who can prescribe personalized molded orthotics.
Q. I have been running where part of my route requires me to run downhill and this is causing some leg pain.
A. Avoid jarring the heel by using a checking action on the downhill stride. Use some forward lean and run relaxed. Make your footplant toward the front of the foot.
Q. What are the best surfaces to run on?
A. Soft running surfaces such as grass do not cause as much shock to the body, but they are often uneven and can twist an ankle or throw you off balance. Running on a smooth, dirt road would be ideal, but they are difficult to find. Asphalt surfaces are hard, but not as hard as cement. If you are forced to run on one of these hard surfaces, be sure you have good shoes and run lightly.
Q. I am having problems with my foot at the main joint of the big toe.
A. Surprisingly, one of the most common causes of toe pain is gout. This must be checked out by your physician. If you do not have gout, your problem may be caused by an improper footplant. You may need a corrective orthotic. Check this problem with a good sports podiatrist.
Q. I have been told that jogging more than two miles per day has a tendency to over-develop certain muscles at the expense of others.
A. Anything that is done continuously will develop the muscles, and jogging does seem to increase the strength of the back and hamstrings. All joggers should use the stretching exercises in Chapter 2 in order to keep the proper hamstring and heel cord length. They should also do bent-knee situps to tighten the abdominal muscles, as well as exercises for the front of the leg, such as toe lifts and leg extensions.
Q. I sometimes get black toenails after a long run.
A. It may be due to hemorrhage under the nails caused by pressure on the toes. Check your shoes to make sure they are the right size and that they provide an ample toe box. Dr. Scholl's toe caps are able to help to reduce the pressure.
Q. Should a woman jog during pregnancy?
A. Most physicians agree that if you are already jogging there is no reason to stop for the first few months, unless there are special problems. After about 3 months, it is probably best for all pregnant women to walk even if they were jogging before. If you have been inactive and decide to begin a program after you become pregnant, you should probably limit your activity to walking or some other moderate activity.
Q. What is Achilles tendonitis?
A. It is an inflammation of the heel cord and/or the sheath that covers it.

Q. What causes Achilles tendonitis?
A. It is usually due either to short, inflexible calf muscles or to weak feet. The best way to prevent it is to engage in daily stretching exercises to lengthen the calf muscles. If it is a foot problem, correct the instability by consulting a good sports podiatrist. Excessive amounts of hill running and speed work will tend to aggravate the irritation of the tendon.

Q. Shin splints are hurting my training program.
A. It is not known exactly what is the best way to prevent or treat shin splints, but they may be due to a weakness of the shin muscles compared to the calf muscles. A program to increase lower leg flexibility may help. Refer to the stretching exercises in Chapter 2. Also, a program that strengthens the extensors of the toe and the foot flexors may help. Some strength exercises to use are: (1) sit on a table with the legs hanging and place a weight across the toes and lift it 25 times, (2) place a one-inch rubber strip over the toes of both feet and force the feet to work against the rubber, (3) turn the feet inward while standing; this increases the strength of the arch muscles, (4) stand on the edge of a towel and curl the toes to pull the towel under the foot.

Q. Is it OK to jog with varicose veins?
A. It depends on how bad the veins are. Jogging usually lowers the pressure in the bad veins because the deep veins are being squeezed by the muscles of the legs. Consult your doctor and ask his advice about wearing support hose or panty hose that might assist the circulation. If you have a severe problem, you might consider walking in waist-high water to obtain hydrostatic support and massage from the water while exercising. You could also use swimming or bicycling as your mode of exercise.

Q. When I have to quit jogging because of illness, how much of my conditioning is lost and how long will it take to regain it?
A. There is no exact answer to this question because of individual differences and state of training. It usually takes two days convalescence for each day of illness. Stressful training sessions should be avoided during the convalescent period.

Q. How can I tell if I have cooled down enough following exercise?
A. A good rule is to continue to cool down until the pulse is below 120 beats or so per minute.

Q. I seem to reach plateaus with my training. I make steady progress and then, for no apparent reason, my performance levels off or declines. What can I do about this problem?
A. Physiologically the human body will go through various training stages as it adapts to the stress placed on it. If you are exercising for long periods of time, your performances will often be good for 6–12 weeks and then drop-off. This is a sign that you should back off on your training, not over-work. If you continue to push yourself, the stage of exhaustion (mentioned by Selye) may set in and performance will decrease. This is the cause of "staleness" which occurs with many runners.

Q. What are the effects of sleep or lack of sleep on distance running?
A. Research indicates that either too much or too little sleep can have a negative effect on performance. Each person has a unique optimum sleep requirement which must be determined by trial and error.

Q. Are women really different from men in their ability to run?

A. There are some basic physiological differences that affect the speed potential of women. For instance, women have a slightly lower hemoglobin level than men (13.9 grams/100 ml blood vs. 15.8 grams/100 ml blood), and a smaller relative heart size. These two differences affect the cellular oxygen supply available during work. Since hemoglobin is the oxygen-carrying molecule, a lower hemoglobin level decreases the amount of oxygen carried. A smaller heart reduces the amount of blood pumped each beat, and this reduction limits the amount of blood pumped each minute. Since blood carries the oxygen, the effect is to reduce the supply.

Women also have less muscle mass per body size than men. This decreases their overall power potential, making it difficult for them to compete in short, intense races.

The differences are not all negative, however, and there is some evidence that women are able to metabolize fats more efficiently than men. This may give them an actual advantage in long distance runs where the supply of stored sugar (glycogen) would be a limiting factor.

Regardless of the physiological differences, jogging can be fun and fulfilling for both sexes, and both can use the same type of training program to increase fitness levels.

Q. After some of my hard training sessions, I develop a cough that persists for some time.

A. This may be due to the drying, irritating effect of the increased volume of air on the respiratory passages. Reduce the intensity of your runs for a while, and build up gradually.

Q. What is second wind?

A. It is not known what causes this phenomenon, but it is usually preceded by intense breathlessness, often accompanied by rapid shallow breathing, a constriction in the chest, a slight throbbing in the head, and some muscle pain. As the exercise continues, both the breathlessness and other symptoms are reduced quite suddenly and in many cases disappear, then the person is able to continue exercising with ease. It is probably associated with a point of metabolic equilibrium.

Q. What can I use to build up the worn portions of my running shoes?

A. A good electric glue gun will solve this problem. Make sure you apply only enough glue to build up the surface to the original level. You can cause foot, leg, and body pain by building an uneven surface on the sole of the shoe.

Q. If I donate blood, should I reduce my training?

A. Several research studies have demonstrated adverse effects on performance for up to 3–4 weeks after the donating of blood. A person should reduce the stress of his or her workouts after giving blood. Using the target heart rate will help you work at the proper intensity after giving blood.

Q. What is blood doping? Does it help?

A. It is the withdrawal and reinjection of a person's own blood under controlled conditions to increase endurance capacity. The current literature shows that it does help increase endurance, but there are ethical questions about using this procedure.

Q. Will an increase in altitude affect my jogging performance?

A. Up to about 3,000 feet there will be little or no effect. When you go above 3,000 feet, the altitude will start to decrease in your performance until you become acclimatized. It will take approximately 4–6 weeks to acclimatize to moderate changes in altitude. You may have to reduce the distance you run or the speed at which you run for a few weeks until your body adjusts.

Q. Does smoking affect my ability to jog?

A. Smoking not only reduces the amount of oxygen carried by the hemoglobin, but it increases the resistance to air flow in and out of the lungs. Both factors reduce your ability to do any kind of endurance or aerobic work. Smoking is also dangerous to your health in terms of heart disease and cancer.

Q. Should children run long distances?

A. Experience has shown the youngsters can handle distance running, even the marathon (26 miles), without any difficulty. The problem comes when parents "push" their children to perform. If the youngster likes to run, and is properly trained, there is no problem.

Q. Sometimes during my run, or just after, my ears seem to stop up. What causes this to occur?

A. There is probably a minor blockage of the eustachian tube which connects the inner ear to the nasal passages. Usually no treatment is needed, but an over-the-counter nasal spray may alleviate this condition.

Q. I sweat so much when I jog, I wondered if I should take salt tablets each day?

A. Most runners can compensate for any salt loss, once they are heat acclimatized, by merely adding a little extra salt to their food. Some research indicates that heavy salt intake may accelerate the process of heat prostration rather than offset it. The important factor is adequate fluid replacement.

Q. Will wearing a rubberized sweat suit while jogging help me lose weight?

A. It will cause a weight loss, but the weight loss will be mostly water and not fat. The problem with wearing a rubberized suit is that you will not be able to dissipate heat effectively. This may lead to a dangerous heat illness. The body was designed to cool by evaporating the sweat. Rubberized suits ruin this system.

Q. What are some guidelines to follow while jogging in the heat?

A. The American College of Sports Medicine has published some guidelines for competition in the heat that are helpful: (1) Don't run more than 10 miles when the wet bulb temperature—globe temperature exceeds 82.4° F, (2) In hot weather, run early in the morning or later in the evening, (3) Drink 13–17 oz. of fluid 10–15 minutes before running, and frequently during a long run, (4) Don't drink fluid with high sugar or electrolyte content. Use only small amounts of sugar (about 2 grams glucose per 100 ml of water) and electrolytes (less than 10m Eq sodium and 5m Eq potassium per liter of solution).

Expose as much of the skin surface as possible to the circulating air so as to aid in the evaporation of sweat.

Q. How good are the commercial "aids" and electrolyte replacement drinks I see advertised for hot weather jogging?

A. These drinks differ in their electrolyte concentration but they basically contain sodium, potassium, and sugar. Despite numerous claims in favor of these drinks, they are probably too concentrated to be the most effective replacement fluid. The rehydration drink should be very dilute (less than 1½ tablespoons sugar per 1 quart water).

Q. What is "carbohydrate loading" and does it help the average jogger?

A. It is a dietary regime designed to increase the amount of stored carbohydrate (glycogen) in the muscle cells. The levels of glycogen can be raised by increasing the amount of carbohydrates in the diet; and increased glycogen does help performance in long runs. However, this technique is not necessary for the average jogger. You should realize that excess water is stored with the carbohydrates. Further information can be obtained by reading a good exercise physiology textbook.

Q. Do people in training require supplementary vitamins and minerals?

A. There is no reason to load up on vitamins either before or during strenuous exercise. Although the need for vitamins and minerals goes up slightly during training, the increased food intake provides for the extra needs. A healthy person who eats a well-balanced diet will get all of the vitamins and minerals he or she requires.

Q. Can I change my eating habits to insure that I will increase my jogging performance?

A. The nutritional requirements of a person who jogs regularly are no different from anyone else's. The evidence to date suggests that the optimum diet for anyone must supply adequate quantities of water, calories, protein, fats, carbohydrates, minerals, and vitamins, in suitable proportions. The best way to supply the needed nutrients is to eat a wide variety of foods from each of the four basic food groups. You can get more information about this topic from a good nutrition textbook at your local library.

Q. Is jogging an effective way to lose weight?

A. Research indicates that lack of physical activity may be the real culprit in obesity. Jogging only 30 minutes a day could cause a 30–35 lb weight loss the first year if everything else remained constant. See Chapter 3 for further information on weight control and jogging.

Q. Can I gain weight and lose fat at the same time?

A. Yes. It is possible to lose fat and still gain weight, since lean muscle weighs more than fat. The important consideration is the loss of inches in the waist, hips, and thighs.

Q. What effect will exercise have on my appetite?

A. A person may actually be "too tired to eat," following exhaustive exercise. The opposite is true for a very inactive person, whose appetite may be greater than that of a person engaged in activity. However, these are extremes. Generally, a person's appetite will increase in proportion to the energy expenditure during exercise. This seems to be the body's way of balancing intake with output, thus maintaining its own weight.

Q. Sometimes on an extra-long run, I suffer from the problem of diarrhea.

A. Diarrhea caused by overstress is a problem for many people. The exact cause is unknown, but some of the following suggestions may reduce or eliminate this problem: (1) Start your runs with an empty stomach and bowel (except for fluids). (2) Avoid foods such as raw fruits, nuts, beans, and cabbage which might contribute to gas formation. (3) Reducing your intake of milk and ice cream may also prove to be helpful if you have a milk sugar intolerance.

Q. Should I jog during my menstrual period?

A. The menstrual period should have little effect on your jogging. In fact, most studies indicate that exercise will help to reduce discomfort during the menstrual period. Women athletes tend to have fewer menstrual problems than nonathletes. However, if it bothers you to run during this time, take a fews days off.

Q. What about running in cold weather?

A. Freezing of the lungs does not occur, according to Carl Gisolfi, a University of Iowa physiologist, who says there is no evidence of cold injury to the larynx or bronchi. He found that air inspired at 40° below zero is warmed to 50–60° above when tested in the mouth. The problem is that all air that comes into the lungs must be completely saturated before it reaches the alveoli. The extreme dryness of cold air may lead to cracking and bleeding of the respiratory passages when 50–100 l/min is moved through the bronchi. When jogging in the cold, it is important to protect the hands, head, and feet. Use several layers of lightweight clothing to cover the rest of the body. Also avoid heavy, bulky garments.

Wind velocity is a factor which can have a great effect in the cold. As the wind increases, the chill factor increases. Following is a Table (7–1) which shows the effect of wind on temperature and outlines the "equivalent chill zones of little danger, increasing danger, and great danger."

Q. What are some other safety suggestions for joggers?

A. 1. Stay off busy streets.
2. Use only roads with a safety margin, such as a sidewalk or a wide shoulder.
3. Run on the left side of the road, facing traffic.
4. Don't argue with dogs.

Q. I read somewhere that women shouldn't jog because they may "displace" the uterus or snap ligaments in the breasts causing them to droop. Are these stories true?

A. There seems to be no research justifying those claims. Most physicians acknowledge the positive effects of jogging for women. Most women report an increase in the firmness of the breasts (probably because of the action of the arms which firms up the pectoral muscles). There is no evidence that jogging actually causes problems with the uterus.

Dr. Evalyn S. Gendel reported that women in top physical condition have less menstrual discomfort, fewer backaches, digestive disorders, colds, and less fatigue than their non-jogging peers.

Q. If I continue to jog until I am 65, what differences can I expect in comparison to a 65-year-old non-jogger?

A. Your maximal work capacity (VO_2 max) peaks about age 20, and then declines gradually until you die. At age 65, the average capacity is about 70 percent of what it is for a 25 year-old individual. However, 65 year-old men who jog regularly often have higher work capacity than many 25 year-old inactive men.

Maximal heart rate usually declines about one beat per year from age 70. Training changes this rate to about .7 beats per year.

The amount of fat on the body of 65 year-old joggers is significantly less than on their untrained peers.

Much of the decrease in performance we see in older people is a result of the decrease in physical activity associated with aging. If you continue to jog, you will be one of the "tough old guys" we see in every marathon who charge right by the younger, less well-conditioned men.

Q. I am still confused about what I should drink during a long run in hot weather. I plan to run a marathon. What would be the best drink to maintain the body's fluid level and help maintain energy?

A. There is no doubt that water lost through sweating limits your tolerance to prolonged exercise in the heat. Depleted carbohydrate stores are also associated with decreased performance. Several research studies have shown that fluid replacement during endurance exercise in warm weather will prevent excessive heat build-up (hyperthemia) and will decrease the circulatory stress associated with hyperthermia.

The problem is to find a drink that can be absorbed quickly and effectively into the body. Apparently, the rate that a fluid moves from the stomach into the small intestine where it can be absorbed depends on the concentration of different

TABLE 7-1 EQUIVALENT CHILL TEMPERATURES

Wind (MPH)	Temperature (Farenheit)																				
	40	35	30	25	20	15	10	5	0	−5	−10	−15	−20	−25	−30	−35	−40	−45	−50	−55	−60
	Equivalent Chill Temperature																				
Calm	40	35	30	25	20	15	10	5	0	−5	−10	−15	−20	−25	−30	−35	−40	−45	−50	−55	−60
5	35	30	25	20	15	10	5	0	−5	−10	−15	−20	−25	−30	−35	−40	−45	−50	−55	−65	−70
10	30	20	15	10	5	0	−10	−15	−20	−25	−35	−40	−45	−50	−60	−65	−70	−75	−80	−90	−95
15	25	15	10	0	−5	−10	−20	−25	−30	−40	−45	−50	−60	−65	−70	−80	−85	−90	−100	−105	−110
20	20	10	5	−5	−10	−15	−25	−30	−35	−45	−50	−60	−65	−75	−80	−85	−95	−100	−110	−115	−120
25	15	10	0	−5	−15	−20	−30	−35	−45	−50	−60	−65	−75	−80	−90	−95	−105	−110	−120	−125	−135
30	10	5	0	−10	−20	−25	−30	−40	−50	−55	−65	−70	−80	−85	−95	−100	−105	−115	−120	−130	−140
35	10	5	−5	−10	−20	−25	−35	−40	−50	−60	−65	−75	−80	−90	−100	−105	−115	−120	−130	−135	−145
40*	10	0	−5	−15	−20	−30	−35	−45	−55	−60	−70	−75	−85	−95	−100	−110	−115	−125	−130	−140	−150

Little Danger

Increasing Danger
(Flesh may freeze within one minute)

Great Danger
(Flesh may freeze within 30 seconds)

*Winds above 40 m.p.h. have little additional effect

components in the fluid. There is a duodenal receptor between the stomach and the intestine which responds to the osmotic pressure created by the solution you drink; this allows some fluids to empty rather rapidly, and causes others to stay in the stomach for a much longer period of time.

The principal solute in most of the "athletic drinks" is sugar, and excess sugar has been shown to delay gastric emptying in proportion to its concentration. Dr. David Costill of Ball State University recommends a drink with less than 2.5 percent sugar. He also states that the amount of usable energy in a drink of this type is small and that the extent to which these sugars aid performance is uncertain. Apparently, the body's primary need is fluid, not sugar.

Most of the prepared "athletic drinks" also contain various sodium, potassium and chloride salts to replace the electrolytes lost in perspiration. However, the loss of these salts is relatively small and they probably do not need to be replaced during the exercise bout. These salts can also affect the rate of gastric emptying. For instance, potassium slows emptying; sodium increases emptying to a certain point, then decreases the effect; and chloride probably has little effect.

A relevant study was just reported in the May 1978 issue of *Research Quarterly,* by Drs. Coyle, Costill, Finch and Hooper, comparing Gatorade, Braketime, Body Punch, and water in terms of gastric emptying and carbohydrate contribution. They found that Braketime, Body Punch, and water were emptied from the stomach much more rapidly than Gatorade. This was not too surprising since Braketime and Body Punch both have sugar concentrations less than 2.5 percent. Gatorade, with a sugar concentration of 4.6 percent emptied 40 percent slower but contributed the most carbohydrates.

The important thing is to drink some type of fluid at every aid station so that your body water levels will be maintained. When the water levels drop, the body temperatures rise and then problems begin.

Appendix 1: Typical Heart Disease Risk Factors

MAJOR FACTORS

Hyperlipidemia (too much fat in the blood)

Hypertension (Blood pressure that is too high)

Cigarette smoking

EKG abnormalities

OTHER RELATED FACTORS

Sedentary life style (getting too little exercise)

Family history of heart disease

Type A behavior

Obesity

Diabetes

Appendix 2: Road Race Organization and Promotion

As you become more committed to jogging as an activity, you may wish to become involved in the organization of road races in order to promote this sport in your own community. By following a few simple suggestions, the road race can be well organized and the participants will have an enjoyable time. It is important to remember that the majority of the people who participate in road races are not Olympic caliber runners but are mainly people who wish to face the personal challenge of how well they can perform at certain distances. The majority of the runners will be extremely grateful for anyone who will take the effort to promote any type of road race. The factors to consider are (1) preliminary planning, (2) publicity, (3) laying out the course, (4) help needed for registration and finish line, (5) equipment, and (6) results.

Preliminary Planning   Careful planning can solve a multitude of problems that might arise on the day of the road race. Following is a list of the factors to consider.

1. Distance. This should be partially determined by the type of runner you expected to attract. It would be ridiculous to plan a marathon if the majority of the people in your area are only jogging between 3–5 miles a day.
2. Locale of the run. The runners should be able to find the location of the race with ease, and there should be ample parking for all of the participants. If possible, select a site that has some scenic value, since most people prefer a pleasant surrounding rather than the asphalt atmosphere of city street. Be aware of any potential hazards that might be dangerous to the runners during the race.
3. Time. Choose a day that will attract the most people, and in scheduling the time of the race consider such factors as temperature, traffic, and travel time from the surrounding areas.
4. Divisions. Decide how many age divisions you will have. Be sure to include divisions for each sex. Make sure that these divisions are clearly understood so that no one will be upset because of a misunderstanding.
5. Awards. Many races should be "run for fun." However, if you decide on awards, you must consider what type of an award, the cost of the award, and how many you will give for each division. A survey of active road race participants indicated that they favor having inexpensive awards in each division rather than a few expensive awards.

6. Race approval. Find out if it is necessary to have approval to utilize the site you have selected. Notify the local police of the event, especially if the race is to be run on public streets.

Publicity   An old adage states that it would be hard to have a war if no one showed up. The same principle applies to road racing. You must get the word to the runners. Some of the ways to accomplish this are: (1) check to see if there is a master yearly schedule for your area and get your race on their schedule, (2) go to other races and hand out flyers about your race to participants there, (3) place posters in local colleges, high schools, junior high schools, and elementary schools, (4) write a brief but clear note about your event for the local media. This note should include the following information: (1) name of race, (2) site, (3) date and time, (4) distance, (5) course description, (6) entry fee, (7) manner of registration, (8) awards, (9) address and phone number of a director who can give further information. They will usually cooperate if the information concerning the race is given to them early. It should be mentioned that directors will not contact you; you must go to them.

Laying Out the Course   After you have decided upon the course, test it at least once before you finalize your plan. Run or ride a bicycle on the course at the same time of day and on the day of the week that the race will be run. This will allow you to find out about any hazards or other problems you might encounter during the race.

One of the most important aspects of laying out a course is to make sure it is measured accurately. Runners are influenced by whether they feel the distance was measured properly. The use of a car odometer is a poor way to determine correct distance. It is estimated that odometers over-measure from 1–5% and this is a large error in even a race of 2–3 miles. The most accurate method is known as the "calibrated bicycle method." This involves the use of a bicycle and a revolution counter attached to the front wheel. Calibrate the counter by riding it over a tape-measured half-mile straightaway. Once you have calibrated your bike, you can measure the race distance accurately and quickly. This extra effort will merit the added goodwill that you will receive from the participants.

When you mark the route, don't take anything for granted. If there are any questionable turning points, mark them with a flag, sign, or some sort of an indicator. One way to find out whether the course is easy to follow is to have a fellow runner who is not familiar with the course, jog the course to see if there are any questions in his mind.

Help Needed for Registration, Start of Race, and Finish Line   Be sure to have plenty of help.

1. Registration. Registrars should arrive at least 45 minutes before the published registration time. This will give them ample opportunity to set up registration tables, receive information concerning numbering or runner identification and fees.

It is important to provide a waiver for each participant to sign, releasing the director of the race from legal responsibility in case of an accident. Make sure that runners who are minors have their releases signed by parents or guardians. This practice can prevent problems arising.

2. Start of the race. Have some type of loud-speaking system that can be used to line up the competitors and give last minute instructions. Also, have at least two stop watches for timing the race. Nothing could be worse than having to tell the runners that you were unable to obtain correct times because of a watch malfunction.
3. Finish. The finish can be the most confusing part of any road race, yet by proper organization, you can record the times and finish order accurately and easily. Following is a diagram of what has proven to be a very successful finish procedure (see Figure A2–1).

Make a sheet with the finish place on one side and a space to record finish times next to the finish place. A second sheet would have the finish place on one side and a space to record the entry number next to the finish place. See fig. A2–2 for an example of this sheet.

As the runners cross the finish line at the front of the chute, the recorder writes down the times as the runners enter the chute. Make sure the chute is long enough to avoid crowding of the finishers as they approach the tables at the end.

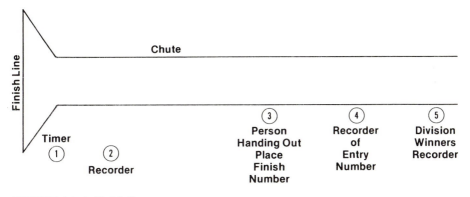

FIGURE A2–1 Finish line.

Finish	Time	Finish	Entry Number
1.	35:06	1.	109
2.	35:08	2.	63
3.	35:09	3.	111
4.	35:12	4.	207
5.	35:14	5.	408

FIGURE A2–2 Finish place sheet.

The first item they will receive is a small piece of paper with their finish place written on it. Make sure you have these papers prepared ahead of time. Many fast-food eating establishments use a numbering system to serve their patrons, and these rolls of numbers serve this purpose. The second person in the chute will record the runner's entry number. The third recorder will check the various numbers in order to determine which are the division winners. He or she can match the numbers with the names on the registration sheets and have the final results before the last runner crosses the finish line. This method has been used in road races with more than a thousand participants; and the meet director was able to award the prizes within two minutes after the last entry crossed the finish line.

Results   The participant is most interested in two things: "how well did I do," and "what was my time." You can quickly provide this information by using the suggested finish line procedure. When you match the two recording sheets, you will have the order of finish, time, and the runner's number. Participants should be reminded before the race to either keep their entry number or to remember it. With their number, they can easily find out how they performed in the race.

A third sheet should have the division winners with their names and times. This information will help you answer any questions and can be used for the press release if you wish to publicize the results of the road race.

For first class organizations, obtain a mimeograph machine to run off individual results following the race, and then everyone will leave with a great amount of respect for you as a race director.

After the race is over, make sure you clean up the area and take down all of the route markers. Remember, you may want to promote the same race next year. Then, while things are still fresh on your mind, write down any suggestions or ideas that might be helpful in planning future races.

Equipment   It does not require much expensive or complex equipment to run a successful road race. The minimum equipment needs are: (1) registration sheets for various divisions, (2) identification system, numbers, cards, name tags, place sticks, etc., (3) stop watches, (at least two) (4) finish and timing sheets, (5) finish and place sheets, (6) finish numbers, and (7) division winners recording sheets. Have plenty of pencils, chairs, tables, clipboards, public address system, and if possible fluids for the runners to drink at the conclusion of the run.

Road races need not be complex. With the proper organization and planning they can be very successful and strongly promote health and fitness through jogging and running.

Appendix 3: Selected References and Resources

BIBLIOGRAPHY

1. American College of Sports Medicine. *Guidelines for Graded Exercise Testing and Exercise Prescription.* Philadelphia: Lea and Febiger, 1986.
2. Allsen, Philip E. *Conditioning and Physical Fitness: Current Answers to Relevant Questions.* Dubuque, IA: Wm. C. Brown Publishers, 1978.
3. Allsen, P. E., J. M. Harrison, and B. Vance. *Fitness for Life: An Individualized Approach.* Dubuque, IA: Wm. C. Brown Publishers, 1984.
4. Astrand, Per-Olof. *Health and Fitness.* Stockholm: SKANDIA Insurance Co. Ltd., 1972.
5. Astrand, P. O., and Kaare Rodahl. *Textbook of Work Physiology.* New York: McGraw-Hill Book Company, 1986.
6. Barnard, A. J. et al. *Cardiovascular Response to Sudden Strenuous Exercise on Heart Rate, Blood Pressure and ECG.* Journal of Applied Physiology, 34 (June 1973): 833.
7. Cooper, Kenneth H. *The Aerobics Way.* New York: M. Evans and Company, Inc., 1977.
8. Cooper, Kenneth H. *The Aerobics Program for Total Well-Being.* New York: M. Evans and Company, Inc., 1982.
9. Fisher, A. Garth. *Your Heart Rate: The Key to Real Fitness.* Provo, UT: Brigham Young University Press, 1976.
10. Hellerstein, Herman K. et al. Principles of Exercise Prescription. In: *Exercise Testing and Exercise Training in Coronary Heart Disease.* John P. Naughton and Herman K. Hellerstein, editors. New York: Academic Press, 1973.
11. Moore, Kenny. The Rules of the Road. In: *Sports Illustrated,* February, p. 59–68, 1978.
12. Pollock, M. L., J. H. Wilmore, and S. M. Fox. *Exercise in Health and Disease—Evaluation and Prescription for Prevention and Rehabilitation.* Philadelphia: W. B. Saunders Company, 1984.
13. Remington, D. W., A. G. Fisher, and E. A. Parent. *How to Lower Your Fat Thermostat,* Provo, Utah: Vitality House International, Inc., 1983.
14. Sharkey, Brian J. *Physiological Fitness & Weight Control.* Mountain Press Publishing Co., 1974. *Step Up to Racing.* Published by World Publications, Mountain View, Calif., 1975.
15. Wilmore, J. H., and A. C. Norton. *The Heart and Lungs at Work.* Schiller Park, Ill., Electronic Instruments Division, 1974.

RECOMMENDED READING

Aerobics, by Kenneth Cooper, M.D.
Guide to Distance Running, From the editors of Runner's World.
The Long-Run Solution, by Joe Henderson.
The New Aerobics, by Kenneth Cooper, M.D.
The Van Aaken Method, by Ernst van Aaken, M.D.

Long Slow Distance, by Joe Henderson.
The Runner's Diet, from the editors of Runner's World.
Runner's Training Guide, from the editors of Runner's World.
Jog, Run, Race, by Joe Henderson.
The Complete Book of Running, by James F. Fixx.
The Aerobic Way, by Kenneth Cooper, M.D.
Conditioning for Distance Running, by Daniels, Fitts, Sheehan.
Conditioning and Physical Fitness: Current Answers to Relevant Questions, by Philip E. Allsen.
Fitness for Life: An Individualized Approach, by Philip E. Allsen, Joyce Harrison, and Barbara Vance.
Fit or Fat by Covert Baily
Jim Fixx's Second Book of Running by James Fixx
The Pritkin Program for Diet and Exercise by Nathan Pritkin
Exercise Prescription For Fitness by J. C. Reid and J. M. Thomson
Strength Fitness—Physiological Principles and Training Techniques by Wayne L. Wescott
How to Lower Your Fat Thermostat. By Remmington, Fisher, and Parent

Appendix 4: Questions and Answers

MULTIPLE CHOICE

1. The proper footplant is to land on the
   a. toes
   b. front two-thirds of the foot
   c. front one-third of the foot
   d. back one-third of the foot   (p. 21)

2. The foot should contact the running surface:
   a. in front of the knee
   b. beneath the knee
   c. behind the knee
   d. approximately 24 inches in front of the body.   (p. 21)

3. The following groups of muscles are prone to lose flexibility due to jogging:
   a. the muscles on the back of the body
   b. the abdominal muscles
   c. the chest muscles
   d. the muscles in the front of the leg   (p. 22)

4. Work done using oxygen is called:
   a. anaerobic
   b. isometric
   c. aerobic
   d. kinetics   (pp. 56–58)

5. Oxygen is carried in the blood by:
   a. hemoglobin
   b. myoglobin
   c. plasma
   d. platelets   (p. 56)

6. The amount of blood ejected each time the heart contracts is called:
   a. heart rate
   b. stroke volume
   c. cardiac output
   d. cardiac capacity   (p. 58)

7. The normal heart at rest pumps approximately how many liters of blood per minute?
   a. 5
   b. 10
   c. 15
   d. 20   (p. 59)

8. A good method to determine your maximum heart rate is to use the formula:
   a. 250 − age
   b. 220 − age
   c. 175 + age
   d. 180 + age   (pp. 14, 58)

9. Which of the following is not a training effect caused by jogging?
   a. increased oxygen uptake
   b. decreased stroke volume
   c. increased number of mitochondria
   d. decreased resting heart rate   (p. 62)

10. The pressure of the blood in the vessels during the time when the heart beats is known as:
    a. diastolic
    b. systolic
    c. pulse pressure
    d. cardiac output   (p. 60)

11. A proper jogging program can increase the maximal oxygen consumption by as much as:
    a. 25%
    b. 35%
    c. 45%
    d. 55%   (p. 62)

12. A training program using jogging as the training method can bring about an increase in:
    a. muscle cells
    b. lactic acid
    c. triglycerides
    d. glycogen   (p. 63)

13. Which of the following is not a good rule to follow in organizing a jogging program?
    a. work out with a friend
    b. run the same distance every day
    c. work out in different places
    d. keep a progress chart   (pp. 64–65)

14. One of the causes of Achilles tendonitis is:
    a. lack of back strength
    b. weak abdominal muscles
    c. inflexible calf muscles
    d. inflexible chest muscles   (p. 74)

15. Which of the following could probably exercise safely without a medical evaluation?
    a. a 46 year old construction worker
    b. a 30 year old teacher who has had some chest pain
    c. a 34 year old insurance salesman who had a physical last year
    d. a 33 year old musician who smokes and is overweight   (p. 1)

16. Which of the following is *not* a good rule for taking the Sharkey's step test?
    a. use a bench 15¾ inches high for men and 13 inches for women
    b. check the pulse at the carotid artery
    c. step at 90 steps/minute
    d. check pulse for 15 seconds beginning 15 seconds after stopping   (p. 7)

17. The guidelines for proper intensity indicate that:
    a. beginners should work at about 85 percent of their maximum heart rate
    b. max. heart rate can be computed by subtracting your age from 200
    c. most joggers prefer to work at about 80 percent max. heart rate
    d. well conditioned joggers work at max. heart rate comfortably   (p. 30)

18. If your target pulse rate for 10 seconds is 23:
    a. speed up if you count a pulse of 24
    b. slow down if you count 20
    c. speed up if you count 21
    d. you really can't tell whether to speed up or slow down   (pp. 16–17)

19. Which of the following statements is false regarding heart rate during exercise?
    a. adults should probably jog at about 80 percent max. heart rate
    b. begin at 70 percent and move to 80 percent as you become more trained
    c. running the same speed at altitude would increase the heart rate
    d. when you exercise in the heat, you must use a lower heart rate   (p. 17)

20. Which of the guidelines concerning duration is incorrect?
    a. five minutes of exercise a day is probably plenty for the average person
    b. at 70 percent max. heart rate, you should jog for about 25 minutes a day
    c. at 80–85 percent max heart rate, 15 to 20 minutes of exercise a day would yield
       a fine training effect
    d. duration over 1 hour is probably not needed except by those who race   (p. 17)

21. Cooling down:
    a. is of little importance
    b. may increase muscle soreness
    c. helps maintain blood flow
    d. none of the above   (p. 18)

22. The Anaerobic threshold:
    a. represents a limit for continuous work
    b. is of little importance in running long distances
    c. will get lower as you train
    d. is extremely dangerous to have   (p. 36)

23. Percent body fat:
    a. can be easily estimated from total body weight
    b. of more than 10% is considered obese
    c. on distance runners may be as low as 10% for females and 6% for males
    d. increases with exercise   (p. 38)

24. Exercise is necessary for a sound weight loss program because:
    a. the loss is primarily fat when exercise is used
    b. the long term effect of exercise results in a significant amount of fat loss
    c. the set point comes down with exercise
    d. all of the above   (pp. 44–45)

COMPLETION

1. The key to a person's jogging program is the selection of ＿＿＿＿＿＿＿ . (p. 2)

2. When purchasing a jogging shoe, the critical features to examine are the ＿＿＿＿ , ＿＿＿＿＿ , ＿＿＿＿＿ , and ＿＿＿＿＿ of the shoe.   (pp. 2–5)

3. In order to reduce the stress on the legs, the ＿＿＿＿＿ of the shoe should be elevated.   (p. 3)

4. The major recommendation in choosing shorts and a shirt for jogging is to select clothing that is ＿＿＿＿＿＿＿ and ＿＿＿＿＿＿＿ .   (p. 5)

5. An easy rule to follow to determine if you are jogging too fast is whether you can ＿＿＿＿＿＿＿＿＿＿＿＿＿ .   (p. 30)

6. In order to utilize fuel for energy in the human cell, ＿＿＿＿＿ is used. (p. 56)

7. In order to obtain training results you must ＿＿＿＿＿ the body system.
                                                            (p. 56)

8. When running up hill you should be relaxed and swing the arms ＿＿＿＿＿ to your direction of movement.   (p. 70)

9. A good substance to reduce chafing between the legs is ＿＿＿＿＿＿＿ .
                                                            (p. 72)

TRUE AND FALSE

1. Canvas shoes make excellent jogging shoes.   (p. 2)
2. The middle sole of the shoe should be soft and pliable.   (p. 3)
3. When buying a jogging shoe a good guide to follow is to purchase the same type of shoe worn by world-class runners in competition.   (p. 2)
4. The key parts of the body to keep warm are the arms, legs, and trunk.   (p. 5)
5. According to Coach Bill Bowerman, the pelvic position is the key to correct jogging posture.   (p. 20)
6. A common mistake made by beginning joggers is running on the toes.   (p. 21)
7. You can conserve energy by using a long stride in jogging.   (p. 21)
8. Excessive noise caused by the footplant is a good indicator of inefficient jogging.
                                                            (p. 21)
9. Joggers are normally quite flexible and thus suffer from few flexibility problems.
                                                            (p. 22)
10. The best type of stretching is a slow, sustained stretching movement.   (p. 22)
11. Since jogging is a relatively easy activity anyone can begin to jog without any problem.   (p. 30)
12. The warm-up and warm-down periods are important aspects of any jogging program.   (pp. 18–19)
13. While jogging you should normally be able to carry on a conversation.   (p. 32)
14. Aerobic is defined as "with oxygen."   (pp. 56–58)
15. The heart is a muscle and will respond to training like any other muscle in the body.   (p. 56)
16. During very intense work the heart may eject as much as 30 liters of blood per minute.   (p. 59)
17. The increased load of blood during contraction is thought to be the stimulus that causes the heart muscle to become stronger.   (p. 56)

18. In order to overload the heart it is necessary to engage in maximum exercise. (p. 56)
19. Jogging will decrease the size of the ventricle. (p. 58)
20. The normal person breathes about 72 times per minute when jogging. (p. 60)
21. One of the results of a jogging program is an increase in the maximum heart rate. (p. 58)
22. An untrained heart cannot completely empty the ventricle each time it beats during maximum work. (p. 62)
23. Jogging is a good method to reduce body fat. (p. 45)
24. Using jogging as a training program decreases the amount of glycogen in the body. (p. 63)
25. When running up hill you should lean into the hill. (p. 70)
26. When running down hill you should lean backward. (p. 70)
27. By limiting your water intake while jogging, you will train the body to reduce the need for water. (p. 77)
28. Children can benefit from a jogging program. (p. 76)
29. Young healthy people can probably begin jogging safely without a physical examination. (p. 2)
30. A person over 45 years of age should probably have a medical evaluation before any major increase in physical activity. (p. 2)
31. A fitness test is a valuable tool to help decide the best level of activity. (p. 6)
32. A person who is already jogging regularly could use the Cooper's test to check his fitness level. (p. 6)
33. The advantage of the "step" test of fitness is that it is submaximal, and can be used by less active people safely. (p. 6)
34. There is no need to adjust the heart rate to age when using the Sharkey's step test. (pp. 8, 9)
35. If you experience excessive fatigue, shortness of breath, light headedness, nausea, or pain in the chest while taking a fitness test, stop the test. (p. 10)
36. Intensity of jogging refers to how long you jog. (p. 13)
37. Athletes often work at higher intensities than would be best for joggers. (p. 13)
38. The relationship between percent of maximum aerobic capacity and percent maximum heart rate is fairly consistent for both well trained and poorly trained people. (p. 13)
39. Checking heart rate at the neck may cause the heart rate to slow down. (p. 15)
40. When you become more trained, you will use 80 percent max heart rate instead of 70 percent as your target. (p. 14)
41. As you become more fit, you will have to run faster to get the same heart rate. (p. 17)
42. Duration is inversely related to intensity; the less intense the exercise, the longer you should run. (p. 17)
43. Jogging once or twice a week is plenty to cause a training effect. (p. 18)
44. Five jogging sessions a week are better than three. (p. 18)
45. If you exercise every other day instead of daily, you should increase the duration. (p. 18)
46. Warming up before jogging is not very important. (pp. 18–19)
47. Cooling down following a jog allows the muscles to continue to help circulate blood. (pp. 18–19)
48. You should probably ignore the intensity of exercise for the first two weeks while you toughen the muscle skeletal system slowly. (p. 30)
49. The typical approach to weight control is the "fad" diet. (p. 38)
50. The terms "overweight" and "overfat" mean the same thing. (p. 38)
51. Women normally have more fat than men. (p. 38)

52. The basic secret of weight control is to jog regularly and to decrease fats and sugars.   (p. 48)
53. A successful weight control program should be adaptable for life long use. (p. 44)
54. There are really no "miracle foods" that will help a jogger perform better. (p. 50)
55. Extra protein is important for a jogger since muscles are broken down.   (p. 54)
56. Carbohydrates are a more efficient fuel for energy than fat.   (p. 54)
57. The amount of energy stored as fat is much greater than from any other source.
                                                                                              (p. 54)
58. Special diets stressing increased amounts of carbohydrates are not necessary for those who jog less than an hour.   (p. 53)
59. One of the changes associated with training is the increased ability to use fats for energy.   (p. 54)

ANSWERS TO EVALUATION QUESTIONS

Page	Answer and Page Reference
	No answer
	No answer
10	Age of person, date and outcome of last medical examination, exercise habits, and whether there is a history of heart disease or presence of major heart disease risk factors. (pp. 1–2)
18	Jog at about 70% rate, 15–25 minutes per day, a minimum of three times per week, gradually increasing to a longer time and eventually to a faster pace. High altitude and intense heat increase the energy required. (p. 17)
19	Cooling down permits the large leg muscles to assist the heart while the blood flow returns to normal volume, helps in removing waste products from the muscles, and may reduce muscle soreness. (pp. 18–19)
23	Receptors in the muscles are stimulated and cause the muscles to contract to resist the stretch. (p. 22)
32	City blocks; advantages—convenience and easily measured distance; disadvantages—most stress on muscles and joints and traffic. Track: advantages—safest, most comfortable surface, and measured distance; disadvantages—sameness of situation and possibly location. Open country: advantages—change of scenery and terrain; disadvantages—less certain footing and possibly location. Hilly, open country is the most challenging. (Partial answer pp. 32, 64, 70)
37	It is the point at which the aerobic systems cannot supply enough energy to maintain the work load. (p. 36)
	No answer
44	Exercise resets the fat thermostat to a lower level, helps to maintain lean body mass, and increases the supply of fat-burning enzymes. (pp. 44–45)
	No answer
52	An increased consumption of fiber foods (whole-grain breads and cereals, fruits, and vegetables) is recommended as is a decrease in foods high in sugar, sodium, and fat. (pp. 48–49)
53	If the sugar concentration in an "aid" drink is greater than about 2.0%, dehydration may result from the slow movement of the fluid into the system. An "aid" drink may also cause a super-saturation of electrolytes. (p. 53)
60	Breathing rate increases from 10–15 times per minute at rest to 45–60 times. Tidal volume increases from about one-half liter to one-half of vital capacity. (p. 60)
60	The goblet cells, which add water to saturate the air as it comes into contact with the inner body, may become overloaded and unable to produce enough mucous to meet the demand. (p. 60)

Page	Answer and Page Reference
60	Trained individuals have a lower heart rate at rest and at steady workloads, a greater aerobic capacity, and greater stroke volume. Minor differences between the trained and untrained are in respect to maximum heart rate and diastolic blood pressure. (p. 58)
64	Your body tells you whether to push yourself, to follow your normal program, or to do less than usual, perhaps even rest. Listlessness, fatigue, soreness, or other pain are signals to back off. (p. 64)
70	You should slow down to a rate of 6.8 miles per hour. (p. 70)

QUESTION ANSWER KEY

Multiple Choice

1. d	9. b	17. c
2. b	10. b	18. c
3. a	11. a	19. d
4. c	12. d	20. a
5. a	13. b	21. c
6. b	14. c	22. a
7. a	15. c	23. c
8. b	16. b	24. d

Completion

1. shoes
2. sole, inside of shoe, heel, and weight
3. heel
4. loose fitting and comfortable
5. carry on a conversation while jogging
6. oxygen
7. overload
8. parallel
9. petroleum jelly

True and False

1. F	13. T	25. T	37. T	49. T
2. T	14. T	26. F	38. T	50. F
3. F	15. T	27. F	39. T	51. T
4. F	16. T	28. T	40. T	52. T
5. T	17. T	29. T	41. T	53. T
6. T	18. F	30. T	42. T	54. T
7. F	19. F	31. T	43. F	55. F
8. T	20. F	32. T	44. T	56. T
9. F	21. F	33. T	45. T	57. T
10. T	22. T	34. F	46. F	58. T
11. F	23. T	35. T	47. T	59. T
12. T	24. F	36. F	48. T	

Index

TABLE 2–2 16-WEEK PROGRESS CHART

		Suggested Time	Actual Time	Dist.	Average Heart Rate	How I Felt
M		20				
T		20				
W	Week 1	25				
T		20				
F		20				
S		27				
M		25				
T		25				
W	Week 2	30				
T		25				
F		27				
S		30				
M		30				
T		25				
W	Week 3	35				
T		30				
F		25				
S		35				
M		30				
T		30				
W	Week 4	25				
T		35				
F		30				
S		30				
M		30				
T		30				
W	Week 5	30				
T		30				
F		30				
S		30				
M		35				
T		20				
W	Week 6	40				
T		30				
F		25				
S		30				
M		35				
T		20				
W	Week 7	40				
T		30				
F		25				
S		30				
M		40				
T		25				
W	Week 8	30				
T		Rest				
F		40				
S		45				

TABLE 2–2—CONTINUED

		Suggested Time	Actual Time	Dist.	Average Heart Rate	How I Felt
M		30				
T		25				
W	Week 9	35				
T		30				
F		25				
S		35				
M		40				
T		25				
W	Week 10	30				
T		Rest				
F		40				
S		45				
M		30				
T		25				
W	Week 11	35				
T		20				
F		25				
S		35				
M		35				
T		35				
W	Week 12	35				
T		35				
F		35				
S		35				
M		35				
T		35				
W	Week 13	35				
T		Rest				
F		55				
S		50				
M		60				
T		Rest				
W	Week 14	60				
T		Rest				
F		60				
S		30				
M		60				
T		Rest				
W	Week 15	60				
T		Rest				
F		60				
S		30				
M		90				
T		Rest				
W	Week 16	30				
T		60				
F		Rest				
S		60				

TABLE 2–2 16-WEEK PROGRESS CHART

		Suggested Time	Actual Time	Dist.	Average Heart Rate	How I Felt
M		20				
T		20				
W	Week 1	25				
T		20				
F		20				
S		27				
M		25				
T		25				
W	Week 2	30				
T		25				
F		27				
S		30				
M		30				
T		25				
W	Week 3	35				
T		30				
F		25				
S		35				
M		30				
T		30				
W	Week 4	25				
T		35				
F		30				
S		30				
M		30				
T		30				
W	Week 5	30				
T		30				
F		30				
S		30				
M		35				
T		20				
W	Week 6	40				
T		30				
F		25				
S		30				
M		35				
T		20				
W	Week 7	40				
T		30				
F		25				
S		30				
M		40				
T		25				
W	Week 8	30				
T		Rest				
F		40				
S		45				

TABLE 2–2—CONTINUED

		Suggested Time	Actual Time	Dist.	Average Heart Rate	How I Felt
M	Week 9	30				
T		25				
W		35				
T		30				
F		25				
S		35				
M	Week 10	40				
T		25				
W		30				
T		Rest				
F		40				
S		45				
M	Week 11	30				
T		25				
W		35				
T		20				
F		25				
S		35				
M	Week 12	35				
T		35				
W		35				
T		35				
F		35				
S		35				
M	Week 13	35				
T		35				
W		35				
T		Rest				
F		55				
S		50				
M	Week 14	60				
T		Rest				
W		60				
T		Rest				
F		60				
S		30				
M	Week 15	60				
T		Rest				
W		60				
T		Rest				
F		60				
S		30				
M	Week 16	90				
T		Rest				
W		30				
T		60				
F		Rest				
S		60				

TABLE 2–2 16-WEEK PROGRESS CHART

		Suggested Time	Actual Time	Dist.	Average Heart Rate	How I Felt
M		20				
T		20				
W	Week 1	25				
T		20				
F		20				
S		27				
M		25				
T		25				
W	Week 2	30				
T		25				
F		27				
S		30				
M		30				
T		25				
W	Week 3	35				
T		30				
F		25				
S		35				
M		30				
T		30				
W	Week 4	25				
T		35				
F		30				
S		30				
M		30				
T		30				
W	Week 5	30				
T		30				
F		30				
S		30				
M		35				
T		20				
W	Week 6	40				
T		30				
F		25				
S		30				
M		35				
T		20				
W	Week 7	40				
T		30				
F		25				
S		30				
M		40				
T		25				
W	Week 8	30				
T		Rest				
F		40				
S		45				

TABLE 2–2—CONTINUED

		Suggested Time	Actual Time	Dist.	Average Heart Rate	How I Felt
M	Week 9	30				
T		25				
W		35				
T		30				
F		25				
S		35				
M	Week 10	40				
T		25				
W		30				
T		Rest				
F		40				
S		45				
M	Week 11	30				
T		25				
W		35				
T		20				
F		25				
S		35				
M	Week 12	35				
T		35				
W		35				
T		35				
F		35				
S		35				
M	Week 13	35				
T		35				
W		35				
T		Rest				
F		55				
S		50				
M	Week 14	60				
T		Rest				
W		60				
T		Rest				
F		60				
S		30				
M	Week 15	60				
T		Rest				
W		60				
T		Rest				
F		60				
S		30				
M	Week 16	90				
T		Rest				
W		30				
T		60				
F		Rest				
S		60				